Aligning Economic and Social Goals in Emerging Economies

Indian Council of
Social Science Research

IDRC | CRDI

Aligning Economic and Social Goals in Emerging Economies

Employment and Social Protection in Brazil, China, India and South Africa

Editor

Gerry Rodgers

INSTITUTE FOR HUMAN DEVELOPMENT
NEW DELHI

www.ihdindia.org

ACADEMIC FOUNDATION
NEW DELHI

www.academicfoundation.com

First published in 2013
by

ACADEMIC FOUNDATION
4772-73 / 23 Bharat Ram Road, (23 Ansari Road),
Darya Ganj, New Delhi - 110 002 (India).
Phones : 23245001 / 02 / 03 / 04.
Fax : +91-11-23245005.
E-mail : books@academicfoundation.com
www.academicfoundation.com

in association with the
Institute for Human Development, New Delhi

Cataloging in Publication Data--DK
Courtesy: D.K. Agencies (P) Ltd. <docinfo@dkagencies.com>

Aligning economic and social goals in emerging economies : employment and social protection in Brazil, China, India and South Africa / editor, Gerry Rodgers.
p. cm.
ISBN 13: 9788171889938
ISBN 10: 817188993X

1. Manpower policy--BRIC countries--Congresses. 2. Economic development--BRIC countries--Congresses. 3. BRIC countries--Economic policy--Congresses. 4. BRIC countries--Social policy--Congresses. I. Rodgers, Gerry. II. Institute for Human Development (New Delhi, India)

DDC 331.11091724 23

Typeset by Italics India, New Delhi.

Printed and bound by The Book Mint, New Delhi.
www.thebookmint.in

Contents

List of Acronyms

AAG:	Average Annualized Growth Rate (South Africa)
ANC:	African National Congress (South Africa)
APL:	Above the Poverty Line (India)
BNDES:	Banco Nacional de Desenvolvimento Econômico e Social (National Bank of Economic and Social Development) (Brazil)
BPC:	Continuous Instalment Benefit (Brazil)
BPL:	Below the Poverty Line (India)
BRICS Countries:	Brazil, Russia, India, China, South Africa
CDRF:	China Development Research Foundation (China)
CSO:	Central Statistical Office (India)
CSP:	Community, Social and Personal Services (South Africa)
EAP:	Economically Active Population (Brazil)
FDI:	Foreign Direct Investment
FET:	Further Education and Training (South Africa)
FSA:	Food Security Act (India)
GDP:	Gross Domestic Product
GET:	General Education and Training (South Africa)
GVA:	Gross Value Added
IADB:	Inter-American Development Bank

IBGE:	Instituto Brasileiro de Geografia e Estatística (Brazilian Institute of Geography and Statistics) (Brazil)
ICSSR:	Indian Council for Social Science Research (India)
IES:	Income and Expenditure Survey (South Africa)
IHD:	Institute for Human Development (India)
ILO:	International Labour Organization
IMF:	International Monetary Fund
IPEA:	Instituto de Pesquisas Econômicas Aplicadas (Institute of Applied Economic Research) (Brazil)
LFS:	Labour Force Survey (South Africa)
MGNREGA:	Mahatma Gandhi National Rural Employment Guarantee Act (India)
MGNREGS:	Mahatma Gandhi National Rural Employment Guarantee Scheme (India)
NBS:	National Bureau of Statistics (China)
NCEUS:	National Commission for Enterprises in the Unorganized Sector (India)
NCMS:	New Co-operative Medical Scheme (China)
NDP:	Net Domestic Product
NGO:	Non-Governmental Organization (India)
NIEs:	New Industrialized Economies
NSS:	National Sample Survey (India)
NSSO:	National Sample Survey Organization (India)
OECD:	Organization for Economic Cooperation and Development
OHS:	October Household Survey (South Africa)
OLS:	Ordinary Least Squares
PBF:	Family Allowance Programme (Brazil)

PETI:	Programme for the Eradication of Child Labour (Brazil)
QLFS:	Quarterly Labour Force Survey (South Africa)
RB&P:	Retirement Benefits & Pensions (Brazil)
SIC:	Standard Industrial Classification (South Africa)
SOEs:	State Owned Enterprises (China)
UI:	Unemployment Insurance (Brazil)
UPAS:	Usual Principal Activity Status (India)
USAS:	Usual Subsidiary Activity Status (India)
USD:	US Dollar
UWSSA:	Unorganized Workers' Social Security Act (India)
WTO:	World Trade Organization

Contributors

Alexandre de Freitas Barbosa, Professor of Economics and Economic History, Institute of Brazilian Studies, University of São Paulo (IEB/USP).

Haroon Bhorat, Director and Professor, Development Policy Research Unit, School of Economics, University of Cape Town.

S. Mahendra Dev, Director, Indira Gandhi Institute of Development Research, Mumbai.

Ajit K. Ghose, Honorary Professor, Institute for Human Development, New Delhi.

Bhajan S. Grewal, Professorial Fellow, Centre for Strategic Economic Studies, Victoria University, Melbourne, Australia.

Rizwanul Islam, Former Special Adviser, Employment Sector, International Labour Office, Geneva, Switzerland.

Natasha Mayet, Researcher, Development Policy Research Unit, School of Economics, University of Cape Town.

Dipak Mazumdar, Senior Research Associate, Munk Centre for International Studies, University of Toronto, Canada.

Amilton Moretto, Professor, Institute of Economics, University of Campinas (IE-UNICAMP), Brazil and Researcher, Centre for Studies in Unionism and Labour Economics.

Gerry Rodgers, Visiting Professor, Institute for Human Development, New Delhi, and former Director, International Institute for Labour Studies, Geneva.

Carlene van der Westhuizen, Senior Researcher, Development Policy Research Unit, School of Economics, University of Cape Town.

Barbara Harriss-White, Professor of Development Studies, University of Oxford, Oxford.

Du Yang, Chief, Division of Labour and Human Capital, Institute of Population and Labour Economics, Chinese Academy of Social Sciences, Beijing.

Foreword

Brazil, China, India and South Africa are not only major new forces in the global economy; they are also important and growing centres of research and policy innovation. In particular, these four countries have all set themselves the goal of developing new approaches to labour and social problems which are consistent with their development strategies. They have different labour market structures, institutions and histories, and different political and economic environments. Yet, even within these different environments, they face similar challenges, and the solutions they are inventing have elements in common as well as features that are different. Much can be learnt by analyzing and comparing the different policy and research approaches emerging in each country.

That was the starting point for this volume, which was conceived at a panel discussion organized by the Indian Council of Social Science Research (ICSSR) and Institute for Human Development (IHD) with support from the International Development Research Centre (IDRC) during the ISLE's 52nd Conference in Dharwad, Karnataka, India, on 16 December, 2010. The panel contrasted experiences in Brazil, China, India and South Africa with respect to labour market trends and social protection strategies, looking for similarities and differences, and examining the policy choices made and their consequences. The panel itself was seen as the first step in a longer term process of collaboration among researchers and research networks from centres in the countries concerned. To that end, the Brazilian Association for Labour Studies (ABET), which—like the ISLE—brings together a large numbers of researchers and policy makers concerned with labour and social issues, is continuing the debate and the dialogue at its next regular conference in Joao Pessoa, Brazil, in September 2011, and the issues will remain on the agenda of future conferences of the ISLE.

This volume consists of papers which were either presented in the panel, and revised by their authors in the light of the discussion there, or written subsequently on the same themes. They describe key features of labour markets and social protection systems in the four countries concerned, their implications for living standards and inequality and the policies adopted in each country to expand participation and protection in fast-growing economies which are engaging with the global economy. Several of the commentators from the panel have also offered short written contributions.

Immense thanks are due to Dr Gerry Rodgers, Visiting Professor, Institute for Human Development and Former Director, International Institute for Labour Studies, Geneva, for not only coordinating this Panel but also very well editing it. Thanks are also due to Dr Edgard Rodriguez and Dr K.N. Jehangir for their active participation in the debate as well as helping in its organizing. We hope that the volume will be a significant contribution to understanding labour market issues in the emerging economies as well as enhancing collaborative research in labour issues between the emerging countries.

Sukhadeo Thorat
Chairman,
Indian Council of
Social Science Research
New Delhi

Alakh N. Sharma
Director,
Institute for Human
Development
New Delhi

Stephen McGurk
Director of South Asia & China
International Development
Research Centre
New Delhi

1 Employment, Social Protection and Equality

Competing or Complementary Goals in Emerging Economies?

Gerry Rodgers

One of the central dilemmas of development is how to ensure that growth is both rapid and equitable. A convincing case can be made that employment is the key: it is through work that the vast majority of people can gain access to the benefits of development. But the employment performance of most economies leaves a great deal to be desired, especially if by employment, we mean jobs done under satisfactory conditions, by workers who are protected against abuse, exploitation, and the contingencies of life, at a reasonable level of productivity, and delivering an income which is enough to reach a decent standard of living. On the contrary, the bulk of the population in low-income countries continues to scrabble for casual work, in informal labour markets, at poverty-level incomes. In some places, open unemployment is high. In others, work is shared in low-productivity workplaces. Dealing with such vulnerabilities calls for effective systems of social protection. But in the developing world, only a minority, and usually a small minority of the population, is protected by formal social security mechanisms.

High growth in the largest emerging economies in recent years now offers the hope that solutions may be found. Rapid growth of output offers at least the possibility of growth in decent jobs, and it should also weaken the fiscal straitjacket and so allow the State more policy space for redistribution and social protection. But a series of structural obstacles has to be overcome, for growth in output is often associated with growth in inequality, competitive pressures continue to bear on wages and incomes, employment elasticities are low, and State action is often misdirected or ineffective.

Under what circumstances can employment and social protection goals be achieved together? What factors impede progress towards these goals? What policy instruments can be deployed?

This volume aims to shed light on these issues, drawing on the experiences of four of the most important emerging economies: Brazil, India, China and South Africa. The notion of an emerging economy is, of course, a loose one, mixing the idea of emergence from under-development with emergence into the light of the international market. This could encompass a wide range of countries, large and small. For the purposes of this volume, we confine ourselves to the Asian giants, India and China, and the largest economies in sub-Saharan Africa and Latin America, that is, South Africa and Brazil, respectively.

The chapters in the book examine the process of development in recent decades in these four economies, and the implications for employment creation and social protection. These countries face some common challenges, notably the challenge of international integration, but there are, of course, important differences among them. In the case of Brazil, the economic and social situation today has been influenced by the labour institutions that were created during the long period of growth up to 1980, then the 'lost decade' of the 1980s, economic liberalization in the 1990s, and the recovery of growth under the Lula Government in the 2000s. In this process, there have been periods of employment growth, notably during the last decade, but also periods of growing unemployment and informality. In China, on the other hand, the key reference point is the process of reform that started in the 1980s and has continued up to the present day, leading to sustained high export-led growth and structural economic transformation. Employment elasticities have been low, but growth has been so high that employment has nevertheless increased substantially. However, a highly dualistic labour market has emerged, with large differentials between urban and rural areas, and between resident and migrant workers in urban production. In India, the process of liberalization that really got under way in the 1990s is the main conditioning factor, but the growth process has been slower than in China and different in nature, leading to very different labour market outcomes. Employment performance has been poor, and the unorganized sector has continued to grow faster than the organized sector, which employs only a small fraction of the workforce. And in South

Africa, the historical break was, of course, the end of apartheid and the discriminations which it embodied in the early 1990s; but the legacy of apartheid remains in the shape of large labour market inequalities and high unemployment. Labour market developments have been influenced by the expansion of international trade, which—unlike in China—has been more skill-intensive than labour-intensive. Employment growth has been too slow to prevent a continuing rise in unemployment, while gaps between skilled and unskilled workers have increased.

All the country studies focus on the period before the current phase of global recession. How labour markets respond to recession is an important part of the story, but at the time of writing, it is still too early to reach conclusions, for the recession is not yet over, and there are considerable uncertainties about future growth paths. In late 2012, there is evidence of weakening growth in emerging economies as stagnation persists in the North. But the data needed to analyse these patterns only become available with a lag. So this book covers the longer period of growth and development during the years and decades before the global crisis struck, including a period of relatively high growth in all four countries during the early years of the twenty-first century, but with much greater diversity of experience during the preceding decades.

The differences among these countries make it clear, if it is not already obvious, that the club of 'emerging economies' is a very diverse group, so it would be naïve to look for general conclusions. On the contrary, it is clear that to understand the pattern of employment creation, one needs focused investigations involving different disciplines: historians to explore the particular development path taken by each country and its consequences, sociologists to consider the social institutions that have emerged, as well as economists to understand the characteristics of the production system and the workings of national markets. The outcomes, in terms of growth and employment, depend on the interplay between these different forces, and that is specific to each country.

However, while generalizations may be risky, it is nevertheless interesting and instructive to contrast the parallel experiences of these four countries, and to attempt to see how common issues have led to diverse outcomes.

What, then, are the central issues?

Converting Growth into Employment

The first issue is to understand the conditions under which economic growth can be converted into a rapid increase in the number of good jobs. On this, each country tells a very different story. In the Chinese study, it is argued that the Lewis turning point is key, that is, the point at which the economy exhausts the elastic supply of labour (at a subsistence wage) from the traditional (rural, agricultural) sectors. Up to that point, high growth may lead to fairly rapid employment increase in the modern sector but wages remain low and 'good', protected jobs are confined to a minority of workers. Once excess labour supply has been exhausted—and it is argued that this point has now been reached—wages and job quality will improve for the labour force as a whole. But if this framework is applied to the Indian economy, we see that while dualism is at least as strong as in China, real wages have been rising in both the organized and unorganized sectors. Moreover the modern, organized sector has been creating very few jobs, and could not be responsible for exhausting excess labour supply. Obviously, the Lewis model does not capture the whole of the story. In South Africa too, the modern sector has been creating too few jobs to absorb an increasing labour force—a gap that emerges as unemployment, in contrast to India where it appears as lower quality jobs in the informal economy. And Brazil has, historically, oscillated between periods of high and low employment creation, but more recently has shown an increased capacity to convert growth into good jobs, largely, it seems, because growth has been accompanied by State policies to increase minimum wages and enforce labour standards. So each of the four countries has a different experience.

The one common element in all four countries is that they are globalizing rapidly. How far does integration into the global market affect the capacity to create enough good jobs? This is an issue on which there is usually more sound than light, but there is certainly a widespread view that poor employment performance has a lot to do with the impact of globalization.[1] Among the four countries studied here, China has clearly been the most successful user of its labour-intensive comparative advantage on global markets, with a rapid expansion of employment in export-oriented manufacturing, while India is at the other extreme, with many believing that international economic integration is responsible for 'jobless growth', in the organized manufacturing sector at least. In South Africa, the demand for skilled labour arising out of international trade stands in sharp contrast to the lack of demand for unskilled labour. This reflects South Africa's difficulty in competing in labour-intensive manufacturing; expanding exports—other than mining—has required a shift up the skill ladder. But this increases inequality within the labour market, as the demand for unskilled workers falls in relative terms. A similar mechanism can be seen in India. And in Brazil, increasing international integration has coincided with a growth of formal jobs, but it is not clear that the latter is the result of the former; on the contrary, it is argued that the high employment elasticity reflects the expanding domestic market and effective State strategy to raise the employment intensity of growth.

Why these differences? They, in part, reflect differences in the pattern of international integration (manufacturing for China, commodities for Brazil, services for India); labour market institutions certainly play some role, less through their impact on labour costs than through their impact on productivity; the size of the domestic market relative to the international market is clearly important (South Africa's market is much smaller than the others); the strategies with respect to technology and sectoral concentration too. Underlying this question is also the 'variety of capitalism' issue discussed in the Brazilian study—the pattern of institutions and socio-economic structures which together generate a particular pattern of economic dynamism and distribution. In some sense, these four countries have four different variants of capitalism, with different roles being played by national and international capital, a different balance of power between labour and capital, and different political structures and labour institutions.

Labour Institutions

So let us consider more specifically the role played by labour institutions. This term includes not only the legal standards applied to work and employment, but also the pattern of organization of workers and employers, wage-setting mechanisms, discrimination, the recognition of skills and qualifications, and the internal labour markets of State bureaucracies and private companies. In all four countries, labour markets are highly regulated, both by the State and by the actors concerned. All have an extensive labour code, but how far it is applied varies widely. In India, the legal framework is fully applied only in the organized sector, covering some 10 per cent of the workforce, though in practice some legal instruments (on child labour or minimum wages, for example) have a wider influence. In China, there is a divide, in urban labour markets, between workers who have rights of residence and others, so that migrants are much less protected. In Brazil, the application of the legal framework has varied with the prevailing political ideology, being weaker during periods of liberalization, and more effective under the progressive government of the last decade. Comparisons between the countries do not suggest any general rule about the relationship between the scope of the labour code and employment, contrary to the general presumptions of market economics. In Brazil, for instance, rising minimum wages have been associated with increases in employment. In India, on the other hand, a weakly applied labour code does not seem to be associated with greater employment levels, though over-bureaucratization may impede employment growth in parts of the organized sector.

In all four countries, trade unions play an important role, and the proportion of the workforce that is organized is high in Brazil, China and South Africa (20 per cent, 30 per cent and 40 per cent of wage workers, respectively, according to ILO statistics); in India, unions are active and visible but their membership is much smaller, reflecting the small size of the organized sector.[2] Labour is organized in different ways across the four countries, so that unions have an important political influence in Brazil but much less so in India, even though in both countries, trade unions have clear political affiliations. In China, of course, the main unions are closely connected with the State. This is also true, in a different way, in South Africa, because of the role of the unions in the struggle against apartheid; but South African unionism is weakened by the extraordinarily high levels of unemployment. The role of unions is, of course, also dependent on the nature of employment relations in the labour market—dominated by casual daily work in India, which is difficult to organize, but by regular jobs in South Africa.

A particularly important 'institution' is the informal economy. Here, there are important differences between the four countries, both in concept and in understanding. In Brazil, the notion of informality, as it is usually understood, is centred on whether or not workers have a signed labour card, an institution which does not exist in the same form in the other countries. The labour card is an important instrument for accessing social protection or ensuring rights at work; those without this card are categorized as belonging to the informal economy. This, of course, only applies to wage workers; most self-employment is also generally treated as part of the informal economy for lack of effective regulation. Historically, the informal sector, so defined, has tended to act as a labour reserve, diminishing during times of economic growth, as during the last decade, while the share of formal work increased. There are some similarities with China, where informality is mainly understood as non-registration, but the context is not the same as in Brazil; most informal workers in China are migrants to urban areas without residence rights, and, therefore, without rights to social protection. Formal–informal dualism is, therefore, embedded in the labour market, though the Chinese study suggests that after the Lewis turning point, it is becoming less important, as the wages of migrant workers rise and the share of informal employment falls.

India is a completely different story. Here, the most widespread concept is the unorganized sector, which is defined in terms of enterprise characteristics, while informality, as used in the Indian study in this book, basically refers to the presence or absence of social protection. Unorganized employment dominates the labour market, indeed the organized sector is declining in relative terms. Meanwhile, South Africa has a surprisingly small informal sector, but this is another legacy of apartheid, which effectively prevented the informal sector from growing. Even post-apartheid, the main adjustment mechanism in the labour market is unemployment, not informal employment.

An important and often 'invisible' component of informal employment is self-employment, as Harriss-White points out in her comments in the last chapter of this book, and this is particularly important in India and Brazil. In India, contrary to the usual assumption that it would decline with development, self-employment has been fairly stable in recent decades at about half of all employment; in Brazil, it accounts for about a quarter. Much self-employment is clearly low-productivity and insecure, but it is studied much less than wage employment, and less is known about the factors determining its level and quality.

Informality is just one aspect of labour market segmentation, which appears in all four countries, between rural and urban areas, between migrants and residents, and almost universally between women and men. South African labour markets are notably slow to emerge from the intense segmentation and unequal opportunity between races that was institutionalized by apartheid. It is essential to understand the institutions that are responsible for such inequalities in order to analyse the relationships between growth, employment and welfare. History is an important part of this analysis, for there is path dependency, and labour market institutions emerge in particular political contexts, and then change much more slowly than the economic environment, so there is often a tension between economic forces and labour institutions.

Social Protection *versus* Job Creation

What then of the balance and interaction between social protection and job creation? The four country experiences reported in this volume reflect different visions and different strategies, but they do suggest that a well-designed combination of job creation and social security provisioning can be a powerful strategy for social inclusion and poverty reduction. However, once again, each situation is different, partly because of the pattern of job creation, and partly because of the type of needs that the social security system is designed to address. In particular, a distinction needs to be made between social assistance and social insurance components of social security. The former basically compensates for income shortfalls which leave people in deprivation or poverty, whatever the reasons for these shortfalls; the latter provides security in the face of life's contingencies—sickness or disability, unemployment, old age, often on a contributory basis. In practice, the dividing line is not always sharp, but there is a clear difference of objective, in the sense that assistance is substituting for employment as an income source, while insurance is making the income stream from employment more secure.

In all four countries, a variety of social insurance measures form part of the standard employment relationship in the formal or organized sector, though the components vary: unemployment insurance is lacking in India, for instance. The main differences come in the coverage of these measures (because of differences in the size of the formal sector, and in the extent to which formal sector firms also use precarious or externalized workers), and above all, in the extent and nature of social assistance. The latter takes the shape of a variety of cash transfer programmes in Brazil, particularly a family allowance aimed at poor households, and the study finds that these considerably reduce the income deficit of the poor. A child support allowance plays a similar role in South Africa. Neither China nor India, however, follows this model. China is building a broad social security framework, within which there is a minimum living standard guarantee, covering over 20 million people since 2002. Initially, this guarantee only applied to those with urban registration; it was assumed that unregistered migrants from rural areas could fall back on family support in their areas of origin. The programme is now being extended to rural areas but some segmentation remains. Meanwhile, India's social assistance framework is patchy, and is mainly based on food subsidies and an expanding employment guarantee scheme, along with a number of non-contributory cash transfer schemes (notably for pensions). The employment guarantee (of 100 days per household) provides an explicit link between social assistance and employment creation, for it assumes that income shortfalls are largely the result of employment deficits.

A key question in all countries is the choice between universal and targeted policies, the difference between a general entitlement and an attempt to focus resources on 'worthy' or vulnerable segments of the population. In practice, some policies are self-targeting (true of the employment guarantee, for instance), while others involve some conditionality in access to benefits based on the characteristics of the population concerned or some desired behaviour (such as school enrolment in Brazil). But the nature of the targeting is different in different countries, its effectiveness is variable, and there are strong arguments in favour of universality.

The studies in this book suggest that social assistance provides an important complement to employment creation. They do not examine the other side of the coin, whether the provision of social protection may raise labour costs and adversely affect employment creation; but that is because the most important forms of protection discussed here are provided by the State outside the labour market, so the question does not arise. Of course, there may be indirect effects on labour supply and wages, but these are surely second order effects at most.

The Pattern of Inequality

All these factors—job creation, labour institutions, social protection—affect inequality. In fact, there are striking differences in the levels and trends of inequality in the four countries studied here. South Africa and Brazil were both highly unequal in the 1990s, but both have made some progress towards reducing inequality. On the other hand, inequality was lower in China and India until the 1980s, but has since been rising rapidly in both countries, as new opportunities were unequally distributed by region, skill and social group. The Chinese study looks for a Kuznets U-shaped pattern of inequality with development, in which inequality starts to decline after a certain point as wages start to rise. But in India, wage inequalities have been growing rapidly, at the same time as wages have been rising generally.

A variety of labour market mechanisms are at work. There are issues of discrimination (by race, gender, caste, migrant status), occupational differentials, returns to education (though wage differentials by education may reflect social hierarchy rather than productivity), labour market segmentation in which different population groups have different opportunities—gender differences are probably the most pervasive—unequal representation and bargaining power, differences in access to policy benefits, and so on. There are inequalities between those with regular jobs, those in casual wage work, and those in self-employment. And behind the inequalities in the labour market are inequalities in the functional distribution of income, with profit shares soaring in India, for example. There are inequalities not only in wages and incomes, but also in conditions of work and security of employment. This takes us back to the labour market institutions discussed above, for persistent inequality in labour markets is sustained by long-lived social institutions.

Brazil and South Africa have both been successful in reducing inequality, but there is a clear difference between them. In South Africa, the labour market has become more unequal as skill differentials widened and racial differentials persisted. If income inequality is declining overall, it is largely because cash transfers are concentrated on lower-income groups, and this redistribution has grown in importance over time. This latter effect is also present in Brazil, but the Brazilian labour market too is becoming less unequal, as minimum wages rise and the share of formal employment increases. In China, the growth in income inequality may now have halted, and the widening scope of the minimum living standard guarantee in China is certainly one reason; wage increases among migrant workers also appear to play a role. Meanwhile, in India, there is some prospect that the employment guarantee programme may slow the rise in inequality, but elsewhere in the labour market, the gaps continue to widen.

All these issues would benefit from more comparative research. This is not simple, of course. When research is carried out in parallel across different countries, as in this volume, points of convergence and difference can be seen, and some comparisons can be made. But in reality, one is comparing systems with many dimensions. The historical origins of the Brazilian model have little in common with those of China, even if some of the problems they face today are similar. So to compare the effectiveness of a particular type of conditional cash transfer in the two countries might not be very productive.

A second important point concerns the database for comparative research. Despite efforts at international standardization, comparable data for many key variables do not exist. Sometimes, this is a conceptual issue. We have already seen the various ways of defining the informal economy. There is a standard international definition of unemployment, but it cannot be interpreted in the same way in each country. Standard disaggregations of occupations or industries may or may not coincide with labour market segments, and there are many variables whose measurement is subject to qualifications and criticisms. Female labour supply is an obvious example. This means that one has to often fall back on qualitative information, which renders comparisons less precise.

So comparative research faces a number of obstacles. This being said, the four broad areas outlined above do merit further research in a comparative framework, perhaps not so much through parallel country studies, but rather by analysing particular issues and relationships in a multi-country framework. For example, it is possible to explore why inequality is rising in India and declining in Brazil by investigating the components of this change in the two countries. Likewise, more could be done to develop broad development models which incorporate the connections between national growth patterns and the global economy, through industrial and financial structures, patterns of ownership and control, and so on, and so tease out some of the employment effects. The main point is to be aware of the historical and institutional contexts, as well as differing concepts and measures, and factor them into the research. Such comparative work should, of course, go beyond the four countries considered here.

All this implies that this volume offers points of departure rather than conclusions; it aims to open a debate rather than to close it. But it is a debate that is important if the economic and social policy agenda in emerging economies is to be grounded in the lessons of international experience.

Reference

World Commission on the Social Dimension of Globalization (2004). *A Fair Globalization: Creating Opportunities for All*. Geneva: ILO.

Notes

1. For an in-depth analysis of this argument, see the World Commission on the Social Dimension of Globalization (2004).
2. Estimates for union membership need to be read with great caution, because of the diverse sources and concepts used. These are orders of magnitude only. ILO data are taken from *http://www.ilo.org/ifpdial/information-resources/dialogue-data/lang--en/index.htm* (accessed on 14 September 2012).

2 Development Pattern, Labour Market and Social Protection in Brazil

What Has (and What Has Not) Changed under the Lula Government?

Alexandre de Freitas Barbosa
and Amilton Moretto

Introduction

This paper attempts to shed light on the interaction between labour market outcomes, poverty and inequality in Brazil in recent years. It is divided into five parts. First, we discuss the variety of capitalism in Brazil, showing how economic dynamism during the period of industrialization (1930-1980) was related to the way in which the labour market was structured, leading to a very unequal, but increasingly complex, urbanized and differentiated society. In the second part, we argue that the opening up of the Brazilian economy brought about a new macroeconomic regime, volatile in nature, which threw the burden of the adjustment onto the labour market variables. In the third part, we show how economic dynamism resumed during the years after 2000, with a strong impact on the labour market. During this period, indicators of poverty and inequality improved, as discussed in part 4. In the last part, we develop the argument that the new wave of cash transfer policies implemented under the Lula government contributed to this outcome. As a conclusion, we argue that this new set of social policies, even though successful in terms of lowering poverty and improving the pattern of consumption of the poor, could not by itself overcome social exclusion or change the labour market structure.

The authors would like to thank Gerry Rodgers for his many insightful comments on the first version of this paper.

Inequality remains as a huge challenge, even with the dynamism of the internal market. The combination of employment growth, reduction of absolute poverty and, at a much slower pace, of inequality, is not enough to bring about a different development pattern. More important still, without deeper structural reforms and new policy instruments, this combination may not be sustainable in the medium term. It depends on whether the internal market can expand on more solid anchors, like rising investment rates and productivity levels, a pre-condition for rising levels of employment and wages.

The Variety of Capitalism in Brazil: Inequality and Labour Outcomes

In recent decades, economics has been dominated by the neo-liberal approach, which defies historical specificities and different social and economic realities. But not all economic theory has been colonized. Boyer and Hollingsworth (1997), for example, point to an interesting paradox, that while economic policy was increasingly following a trajectory built around efficient markets from the 1980s onwards, alternative theoretical constructs, mostly heterodox, were developing at the same time. These drew on the complexity of the really existing markets. The emphasis was placed on connections between markets and a complex of social and economic institutions, responsible for 'the discovery' of various modalities of capitalism. Instead of a single institutional architecture, posited as the most efficient, this approach was built on the diversity inherent to capitalist societies (Amable, 2005). In the words of Gray (1998), the economic modernization undergone by many countries of both the North and South would not replicate the American 'free market' model. On the contrary, the post-1980 period is characterized by the emergence of different types of capitalism.

Nonetheless, instead of the hypothesis that the global market would lead to a convergence of models of capitalism, a thesis embraced by Gray, other authors like Boyer and Hollingsworth (1997), foresee the co-existence of different social systems of production that could interact in the global economy. In this framework, there is neither complete globalization of the factors of production, nor perfect competition in the product markets, coupled with a resistance to transferring modern technologies. Each national economy exhibits a complex organization that varies according to the productive sectors, regional characteristics, power differences between capital and labour, and market organization mechanisms, shaping and being shaped, as well, by the restructured capitalist world economy.

Several studies have been conducted with the purpose of understanding the distinct varieties of capitalism. In addition to investigating a complex of institutions, such studies aim at assessing how these institutions complement and interact with each other. Amable (2005), for example, proposes a model to map the relationships between five institutional sectors—competition in the product market, labour relations, financial intermediation, social protection and education—in the economies of 21 developed countries.

Such studies, however, are largely restricted to the developed countries. The exclusion of the under-developed countries[1] from these analyses may be accounted for either by a lack of knowledge about the reality of the countries at the periphery of global capitalism, or by a conception—misguided, in our view—that these countries have not succeeded in 'endogenizing' the dynamics of capitalism.

Actually, they did, especially Brazil, in their own way. Understanding this process was an important contribution of the so-called ECLAC school, which flourished from the 1950s to the 1970s. In the early 1960s, Furtado (1965) pointed out that the Industrial Revolution had promoted a qualitative change in the development process. In the European countries, and later on in the United States, economic growth seemed quasi-spontaneous, as technological progress opened the way for a growing diversification of production and demand. On the other side of the international division of labour, and especially in the case of the Latin American countries, capitalism only penetrated half way, without homogenizing or completely transforming economic and social structures, while only internalizing new patterns of consumption among the wealthiest. As a result, these economies tended to enter into the dynamics of the global capitalist system without being able to create even a minimally integrated domestic economy. Brazil figured as a paradigmatic case, since the relations of dependency did not prevent the economy from showing great dynamism (Cardoso and Falleto, 1970; Furtado, 1974). The unavoidable outcome was the aggravation of inequalities of income and power, and the deepening of the country's internal regional gaps.

According to Prebisch (1981), this dynamism was circumscribed, despite the periods of rapid industrial expansion and vigorous growth. Capitalist sectors co-existed with non-capitalist ones, engendering a peculiar 'style of development', distorted and heterogeneous. Transformations in the technological structure of the economy produced a partial transfer of the labour force from subsistence to modern sectors, yet wages did not rise to reflect gains in productivity. The economic surplus did not lead to the accumulation of capital; rather, it filtered into conspicuous consumption, non-reproductive capital, and outflows of profit and interest.

From 1930 to 1980, the Brazilian economy proved to be the most dynamic worldwide, expanding at an annual average rate of 6 per cent. During this period, out of a vast rural region emerged the developing world's most advanced industry. The secrets of Brazilian capitalism may be found in the multiple role of the State as entrepreneur, funder, and regulatory agent, spearheading the expansion of private capital, with a predominance of transnational companies in the most dynamic sectors, turning Brazil into a sort of a role model of 'dependent capitalism', very different from the classical dependency (Evans, 1979). Furthermore, the existence of an elastic reserve army of labour would play the important role of ensuring the profitability of capital (Oliveira, 2003).

To sum up, the Brazilian variety of capitalism structured itself on the combination of powerful and selective State action; attraction of transnational companies to the dynamic sectors; existence of a national entrepreneur which monopolized traditional sectors and acted as a subsidiary to foreign capital in all others; vast masses of recently urbanized workers, deprived of rights and performing casual jobs; internal boundaries designed to allow increasing returns on capital with public subsidies; lack of agrarian reform and explosive expansion of the country's cities; the existence of a middle class with high levels of income and schooling; and financial and technological dependence on the economies of the developed countries, which held back a transformation of capitalism towards greater national autonomy.

Brazilian labour market institutions were built after the 1930s, when industrialization started redefining the social and economic dimensions of the country. It was the first time in Brazilian history that most of the labour force came from within its territory—before that, the labour force was mainly furnished by African slaves and then, at the end of the nineteenth century, by European workers directed to the coffee production—mainly from the Northeast, both pushed towards and pulled by the dynamic economy of the Southeast region. A Labour Code was introduced in 1943 and a minimum wage was set in 1940. The ratio of wage-earners to the economically active population soared during the period, as a national working class and a salaried middle class gained ground.

Before that date, the absence of a labour market had hampered the emergence of a dynamic and endogenous capitalism. Brazil had experienced three periods during its labour history (Barbosa, 2003). During colonial times, slavery was predominant, and work was synonymous with compulsory labour. The production of sugarcane, domestic services, mining and craft production were performed by slaves. Hence, there was no labour market, rather a continuous flow of workers supplied by the slave trade. In 1850, this infamous trade was forbidden, inaugurating a 40-year transition period up to the end of slavery (1888). Then, the first Republican period (1889-1930) saw the making of fragmented and incomplete 'regional labour markets'. Wage earners were few in number and workers were incorporated into the production process through personal ties and usually without labour contracts. Agriculture predominated and most of its production was for external markets or aimed at the subsistence of the workers.

After 1930, a national labour market was structured. The level of registered wage-earners grew more rapidly than the Economically Active Population (EAP)—at 6.2 per cent and 2.6 per cent per year, respectively—between 1940 and 1980 (Pochmann, 1998). Throughout this period, while employment grew by approximately 186 per cent overall, employment in the manufacturing sector expanded by 423 per cent, and in government services, even more rapidly, by 527 per cent, according to Census data.

Brazil's industrialization process thus gave birth to a national working class protected by labour legislation, even if not all segments of the labour force were covered. Meanwhile, the salaried middle class expanded—

technicians and professionals with college degrees, many of them working as private and public sector managers. However, despite this creation of a relatively 'modern' labour market, there remained important differences when compared to the employment patterns in developed countries: high income disparities, a high percentage of unregistered wage-earners, a large percentage of the labour force outside the capitalist sector in both rural and urban areas, and the lack of a universal system of social protection.

By the end of this cycle of expansion, approximately one-third of the country's wage earners, in both urban and rural areas, were still out of reach of the labour legislation. If we add in precarious self-employment, domestic servants and the unemployed, this was true of some 35 per cent of the Brazilian labour force in 1981 (Santos, 2002).

During this period, a corporatist union structure was established, which was limited to union registrations conceded by the Government, but collective agreements were scarce. After 1964, the repression of union leaders was common: a majority of the union leaders were removed from their positions, and many were imprisoned. This situation started changing with the new unionism of the late 1970s and the re-democratization process that led to the signing of 1988 Constitution.

To sum up, social mobility could be seen in the creation of a salaried middle class, and some sectors of the working class gained access to basic rights, but functional and personal income inequality increased dramatically. For instance, the gap between the average income of the wealthiest 10 per cent and the poorest 10 per cent rose from 21-fold to 47-fold between 1960 and 1980. Moreover, the country was unable to build a national financial system, and thus became an easy prey to the international oscillations of the late 1970s, nor did it succeed in developing a national system of innovation.

Urbanization was another trend of the period. Between 1950 and 1980, the urban population expanded at an annual pace of 4.4 per cent, leading to an urbanization rate of about 70 per cent at the end of the period. The metropolises concentrated both wealth and social exclusion. In 1980, 58 per cent of the poor were already found in urban and metropolitan areas (Rocha, 2004).

During this long period of growth, the 1964 coup d'etat was an important point of inflexion. Brazil would continue growing in a dynamic way up to 1980, with increasing internationalization of commerce, production and finance. But the political arena changed: there was no longer space for the diverse sectors of society to express their interests. The country was ruled by an autocratic bourgeoisie (Fernandes, 1987), allied to oligarchic groups with the acquiescence of segments of the middle class, while the working majority would now be deprived of the benefits of increased growth and productivity.

The process of expansion was interrupted in the 1980s due to the international crisis. In order to cushion that crisis, the Brazilian Government signed agreements with the International Monetary Fund (IMF) that included raising domestic interest rates and the generation of trade surpluses. Domestic public debt rose in order to cover the cost of servicing foreign debt (Belluzzo and Almeida, 2002). But contrary to the conservative diagnosis, inflation did not fall, while GDP stagnated throughout the decade and urban unemployment levels rose.

Despite the process of re-democratization that led to the signing of the 1988 Constitution and the strengthening of social movements, the 1990s were characterized by the introduction of a plan to stabilize price levels, based on a set of economic reforms geared towards deregulation and liberalization.

In this context, as we shall see in the next section, the social structure and the labour market faced a disorganization process, at the expense of its core workers, who had been assimilated by a very unique variety of capitalism. The rapid opening up of the economy and the changing role of the State—in a global context dictated by financial flows and by transnational investments carried out mainly through mergers and acquisitions—weakened the dynamism of the Brazilian economy, which was no longer able to rely on the internal market and the 'visible hand' of once-powerful State institutions. Brazilian capitalism came to a standstill.

Brazil in the Nineties: Macroeconomic Regime and the Labour Market

In the early 1980s, the Brazilian economy was hit by a great blow. The combination of high international interest rates and oil prices, a drop in the price of all other commodities, and a recession in the developed countries wreaked havoc in Brazil. Unlike the countries of Southeast Asia, Brazil had become hostage to short-term loans extended by international private banks, while the State was, by far, the main debtor.

In the wake of the debt crisis and the quasi-failure of the State, which had to rescue the private sector, rising inflation was one more element compounding the grim outlook forecast for the country. The Government reacted to the problems by devaluing the Brazilian currency and raising interest rates to rein in high inflation rates. The Brazilian economy intentionally went into a strategic recession aimed at generating trade surpluses and honouring foreign debt obligations. Meanwhile, the public deficit skyrocketed, basically as a result of the conversion of foreign debt into domestic debt.

Notwithstanding the fact that investment rates were seriously affected, segments of the industrial oligopolies managed to maintain their profit rates. The various fractions of capital, which had developed during the previous period, started seeking protection in the yields of a financial merry-go-round created by a State that was depleted of resources and highly indebted, while interest rates soared and fiscal advantages were granted by the Government (Belluzo and Almeida, 2002).

As a consequence, GDP per head stagnated between the beginning and the end of the 1980s. Unemployment rose and wages, unable to keep pace with inflation, lost purchasing power. Simultaneously, Brazil, which had succeeded in constituting its industrial park in the late 1970s, was soon outdated in productive terms, now that the developed countries were beginning a new technological revolution and a new wave of 'developing countries' were making progress on catching up with the rich countries.

The 1980s came to be known in the economic history of Brazil and the rest of Latin America as 'the lost decade'. High inflation, stagnant investment levels and a domestic market slowdown were coupled with massive capital transfers to service the foreign debt. Stabilization plans succeeded one another, yet none managed to control the inflationary spiral. At the same time, technological stagnation and a downsized and neglected State apparatus soon took their toll.

It was only as of July 1994, with the implementation of the Real Plan, that the Brazilian economy managed to not only reduce inflation, but also to stabilize it at a lower level.[2] However, the monetary stabilization plan also involved a set of structural reforms in the Brazilian economy. The mentors of the plan believed that they were inaugurating a new model of growth, focused on achieving gains in productivity through privatization, on trade liberalization and on attracting foreign investment (Franco, 1999).

The Real Plan's core instrument was a currency peg that established a band within which the Brazilian real would vary in relation to the US dollar. The goal was to appreciate the real, thus reducing the cost of imports, in order to control inflation and facilitate the modernization of the Brazilian economy. However, as import tariffs were reduced drastically, trade and current account deficits soon went out of control, triggering a hike in domestic interest rates designed to attract foreign private capital. The country's opportunistic financial liberalization, fuelled by an international excess of liquidity, took a high toll on the public accounts, with once again the heaviest burden being shouldered by the Federal Government.

The period from 1994 to 1998 may thus be characterized as one of 'ultra-liberalization', one which generated strong competitive pressure on Brazilian companies. However, given the macroeconomic setting (high interest rates, overvalued currency, tax increases and lower import tariffs), these companies did not respond by introducing new technologies. They preferred, instead, to reduce their product lines, import capital goods and make defensive adjustments through outsourcing (Kupfer, 2005).

As a result, job casualization and unemployment thrived in the 1990s in Brazil, especially after 1995, reaching their maximum in 1999, the year the country suffered a speculative attack and was forced to devalue the real. Open unemployment neared 10 per cent at the national level and informality (measured by the lack of access to social security) exceeded 50 per cent of all those occupied (Figure 2.1).

Actually, it was only after the 1999 devaluation of the foreign exchange rate that Brazilian economic policy changed, now hinging on a new tripod: floating exchange rate, primary surpluses and inflation targets. This meant that any time the currency depreciated, interest rates rose to harness inflation, followed by a rise in primary surpluses. Conversely, currency appreciation made it possible to reduce interest rates and, in theory, to adopt more expansionist fiscal policies.

Figure 2.1

Unemployment and Informality Rates for Selected Years (%)

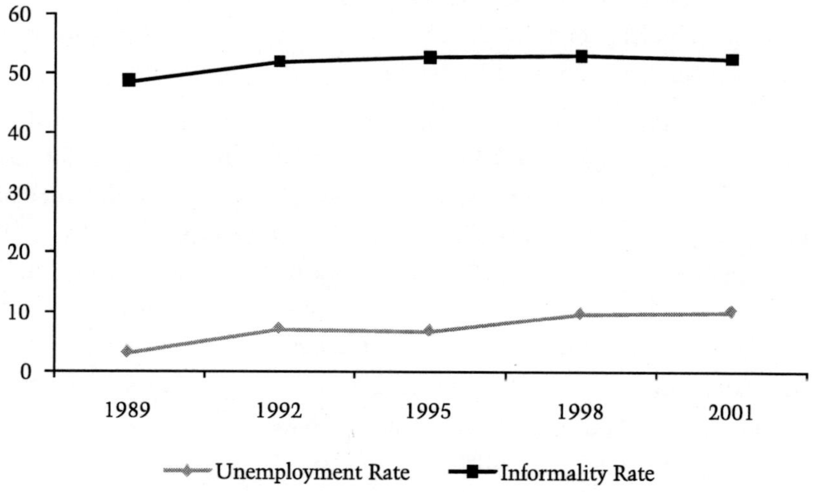

Source: PNAD/IBGE and IPEA.

Throughout the period 1994-2002, Brazil grew at lower-than-3 per cent rates, and in a very unstable way, continuing the stop-and-go trajectory that had started in the 1980s. Each mini-cycle of growth was aborted by foreign deficits, which demanded high interest rates. And the inflow of foreign direct investment (FDI) failed to produce an increase in the overall investment rate, given that it mostly targeted the purchase of assets held by national companies, whether State-owned or private.

In addition to a weakened State, an economy unprepared to grow, high unemployment and informality rates, and skyrocketing public debt triggered by the high interest rates, Brazil modernized in a way that was both selective and lacking domestic technological innovations. The domestic market behaved erratically while in the foreign market, Brazilian companies—except for some islands of excellence—proved uncompetitive because of the anti-growth macroeconomic regime. That is, alongside lower GDP growth, the aggregate productivity of the Brazilian economy also began to expand more slowly, when compared with the more dynamic periods of the 1950s and 1970s (Figure 2.2), when there was a strong expansion of domestic demand, boosted by industrial diversification.

Figure 2.2

GDP and Productivity Growth Rates (Average Annual Growth in %)

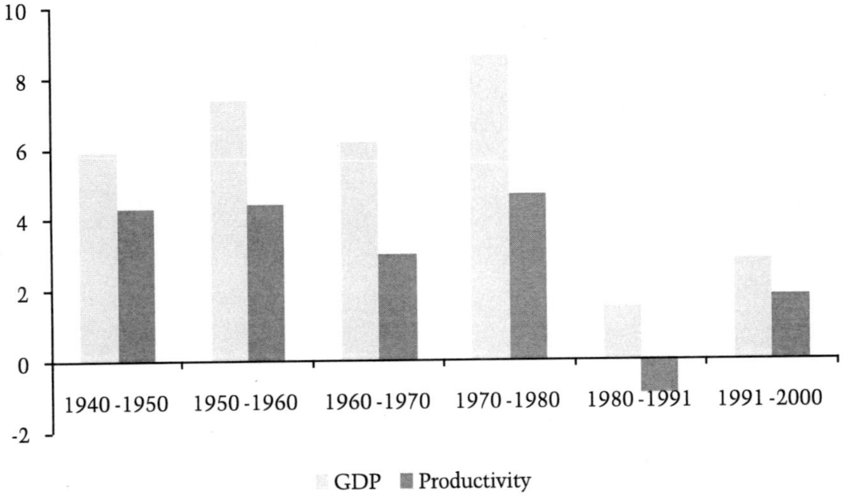

Source: SCN/IBGE and IPEA.

Brazilian capitalism was about to face an involution process, as if it could afford to overlook the need to accumulate capital. Foreign capital was attracted, new consumption and technological patterns were imported, yet these were restricted to a small elite. In practice, this perverse logic of macroeconomic management altered the country's economic dynamics, stimulating the denationalization of the productive apparatus, the valorization of the financial rather than the real economy, and the scrapping of some of the few sources for the development of national technology. Returns to capital, overwhelmingly national and, rather more specifically, owned by former industrialists, came mostly through the financial sphere, both by way of high yields on bonds issued by the Brazilian Government to cover its huge public deficit, and by way of the high margins charged by banks on their loans to companies and households.

On the labour front, at the end of this low-growth period, almost 23 per cent of the country's economically active population could be bracketed as a part of a structural labour surplus (Jakobsen and Barbosa, 2008). Open unemployment did not capture the whole of the worsening of labour market conditions. Even the informality rate (the proportion of workers without access to social security) did not reflect all the different patterns of interaction within the labour market among very diverse social groups.

Looking at Figure 2.3 below, one can notice that the non-capitalist sector and the industrial reserve army amounted to around 50 per cent of the labour force, excluding the employers. There was still an important rights-based working class ('primary market') and a white-collar middle class (with tertiary education), which accounted for 35 per cent of the labour force. In between, there was a large secondary labour market made up of casual wage workers, which grew fast in the 1990s. This structure of the labour market insertion of Brazilian workers helps one understand how the pattern of modernization disorganized further a labour market that was already quite segmented.

Figure 2.3

Distribution of the Workforce by Share in the Labour Market, 2002

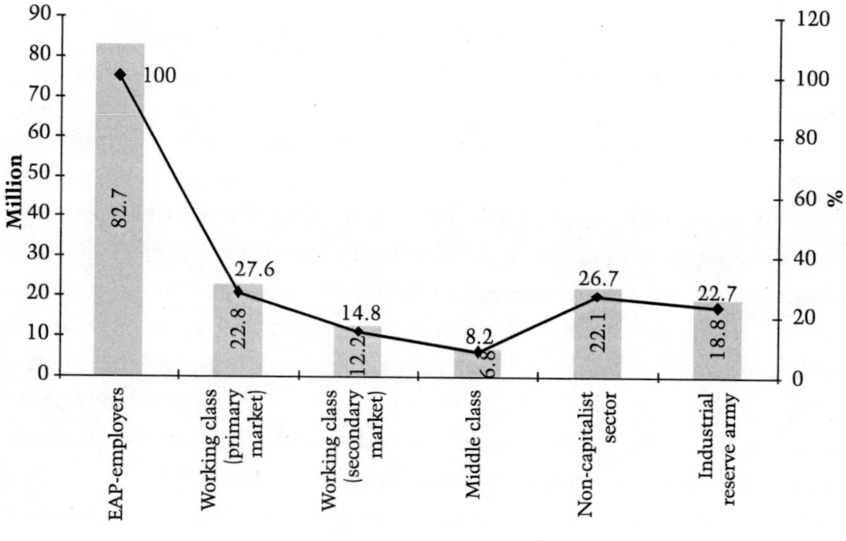

Source: PNAD/IBGE. Categories elaborated by the authors.

Brazil After 2000: Economic Dynamism, Labour Market Outcomes and Development Pattern

After nearly a quarter of a century of economic stagnation, the Brazilian economy resumed growth from 2004 to 2008. During this period,

GDP expanded at an average rate of 4.5 per cent per year, slower than the other BRICS (Brazil, Russia, India, China and South Africa) countries, but twice the average rate prevalent during the last two decades of the twentieth century. It is worth recalling that during the first year of the Lula Government, in 2003, the economy faced a quasi-recession as a result of a strong hike in interest rates, put into place because of the devaluation of the local currency in 2002, which affected inflation levels.

Somewhat surprisingly, one year later, Brazilian capitalism again started showing dynamism, and this time, unlike the stop-and-go of the 1990s, it did not fade away in the short term. Two factors explain the country's renewed growth. In the first place, the international boom allowed for a significant improvement of the foreign accounts after 2002. Foreign debt was reduced, exports more than trebled between 2003 and 2008, and international capital proved more accessible. The ratio of external debt to exports, which had reached 4.5 in the late 1990s, came down to less than 1 in 2008 (Figure 2.4).

Figure 2.4

Exports (A), External Debt (B) (in US$ millions) and the Ratio B/A

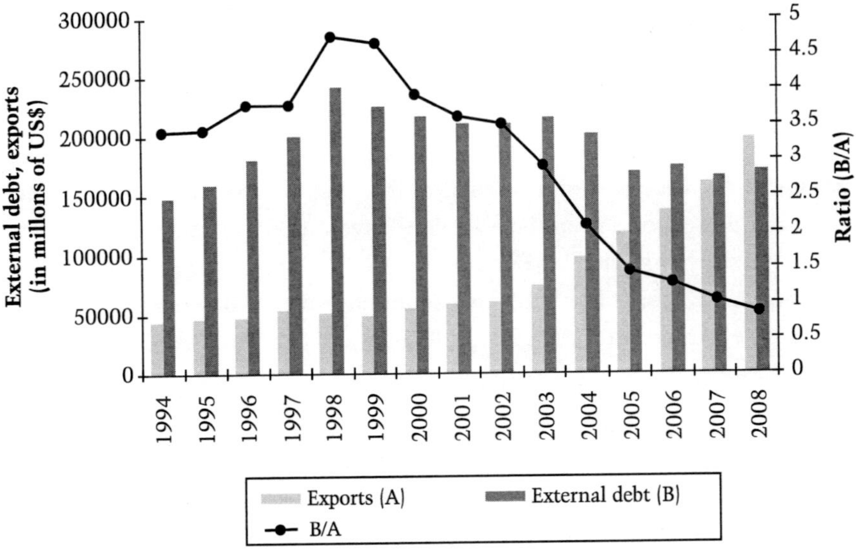

Source: Central Bank of Brazil.

What is more, foreign direct investment (FDI) returned to the country, now in the form of greenfield investments and, in a majority of cases, raising productive capacity. Just as an illustration, Brazil received US$ 45 billion in FDI in 2008, three times more than in 2003.

In the second place, a decrease in domestic interest rates, together with the expansion of credit and public spending—on infrastructure and earmarked for social programmes, including retirement pensions pegged to rising minimum wages—boosted the domestic market which, in turn, brought new hope for private investors. In parallel, companies started facing less competitive pressure, thus enabling the replacement of certain imports by domestic production, in spite of a foreign exchange rate that had started appreciating from 2005 onwards. That is, the country's improved foreign accounts acted as a positive exogenous factor, which permitted the adoption of new internal stimuli. The interplay between these two forces made it possible to reinforce the accumulation of capital, with repercussions for employment levels and wages.

The State's accounts also reflected this setting. Fiscal balance was attained without the need to make cuts in indispensable expenditures and the primary surplus kept nominal deficits from becoming significant. As a consequence, during the recent growth cycle, there was an almost continuous drop in the public debt/GDP ratio.

On the other hand, lack of investment, poor infrastructure, and the need to create the conditions for continuing the economic expansion prompted the Federal Government to, first, resume spending on big public works and, second, stimulate private investment, mainly through its development bank, the BNDES (National Bank of Economic and Social Development), which holds an investment portfolio that is greater than the IADB (Inter-American Development Bank)'s and the World Bank's portfolios added together.

The combination of growth in exports and an expanding domestic market, coupled with an increase in public and private investment, boosted job creation. During the period 1999-2006, employment expansion (2.7 per cent a year) outpaced the expansion of the workforce. Formal employment grew even faster, leading to an increased formalization of the labour force.

This trend was the opposite of that witnessed during the period 1995-1999, which was marked by low growth and strong competitive pressure (Figure 2.5).

Figure 2.5

Annual Growth Rates (%) of Economically Active Population (EAP), Level of Employment (TE) and Formal Employment (FE) for Selected Periods

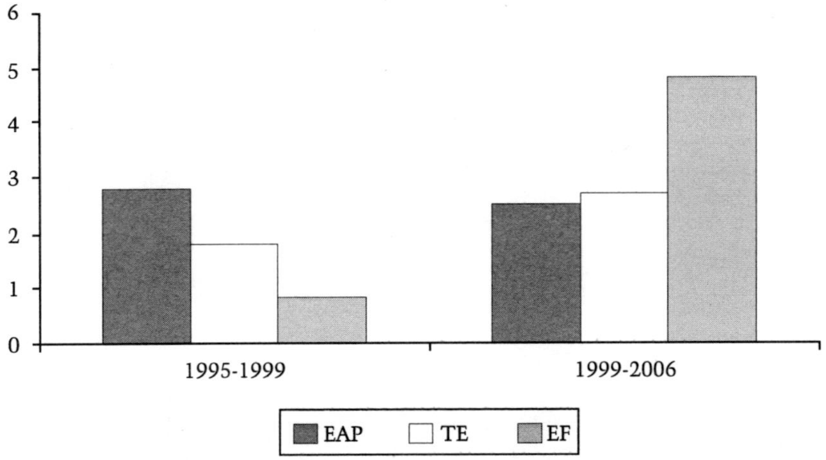

Source: PNAD/IBGE and IPEA.

The open unemployment rate reached its highest level in Brazilian history in the year 2003, after which it fell almost continuously, reaching 6.7 per cent in 2010 (Figure 2.6). When the crisis hit Brazil in 2009, the effect on unemployment was rather small, not really stopping its downward movement. At that time, counter-cyclical measures were implemented and the internal market, already dynamic, maintained the level of growth.

One very peculiar feature of the Brazilian case is the high employment–product elasticity, which has to do with the size of the domestic market, an economy less open to the world—up to 2008, imports made up less than 20 per cent of the apparent consumption—and the linkages fostered among the agricultural, services and industrial sectors in a very urbanized and monetized economy, even in the case of non-capitalist activities.

Figure 2.6

Rate of Open Unemployment in Major Metropolitan Areas (%)

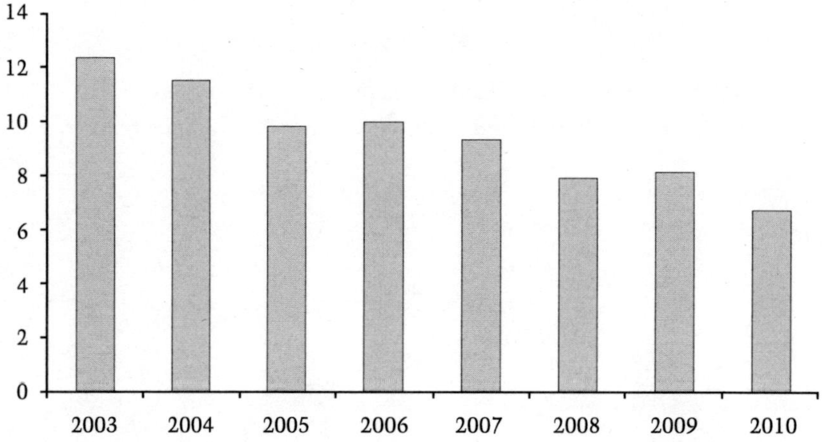

Source: PME/IBGE.

The data presented above on unemployment should be interpreted with care, as the metropolitan areas account for a little less than 40 per cent of the total number of unemployed. Unemployment is falling less rapidly in urban non-metropolitan areas and rising in rural areas, even though starting from very low levels. And the labour surplus is still high, as open unemployment does not capture the entire reality of the labour market in countries like Brazil.

Moreover, the great majority of the formal jobs generated in the country during the period of strong economic growth shared one characteristic in common: the prevalence of low wages. The traditional Brazilian picture of a high concentration of poorly paid occupations can be seen in Table 2.1. A high and increasing percentage of the total formal jobs—over 90 per cent—paid no more than three times the minimum wage during a period where the turnover rate peaked.

Obviously, a part of the increase of the share of workers getting up to three minimum wages has to do with the substantial increase of the minimum wage in real terms, flattening the wage structure in Brazil as the wage floor has risen. However, it also has to do with the increase in the turnover rate—a recurrent pattern in Brazil every time the level of employment grows faster—as employers substitute lower-wage for higher-wage workers, which is possible because of the flexibility of the labour market and the existence of a huge labour surplus.

Table 2.1

Distribution of Formal Jobs By Wage Level

	Up to 3 Minimum Wages	*More than 3 and up to 5 Minimum Wages*	*More than 5 and up to 10 Minimum Wages*	*More than 10 Minimum Wages*	*Total*
2004	88.52%	7.08%	3.13%	1.27%	20,945,705
2005	89.41%	6.53%	2.90%	1.16%	22,968,686
2006	91.23%	5.32%	2.48%	0.96%	24,278,593
2007	91.97%	4.88%	2.26%	0.89%	26,900,025
2008	92.11%	4.83%	2.19%	0.87%	31,662,595
2009	92.71%	4.51%	2.01%	0.77%	31,182,214
2010*	93.57%	3.96%	1.80%	0.66%	24,080,425

Note: *Period: January to July.

Source: Caged/MTE.

Yet if the informality rate retreated, it was still higher than the levels found at the end of the industrialization period (1930-1980). Table 2.2 shows that even though formal jobs accounted for 95 per cent of the increase in employment, they still represented less than 40 per cent of the labour force. Self-employed, domestic workers, unpaid workers (mostly in family enterprises) and subsistence workers still made up a third of the Brazilian labour force (Table 2.2), leading to a labour market structure that is very different from the one found in developed economies, even if the latter have been increasingly affected by informality and casualization of labour in recent years.

During the short period from 2003 to 2008, there was also a dramatic change in the educational attainment of occupied workers. Workers with at least 11 years of schooling (high school or more), who accounted for one-third of the labour force in 2003, raised their share to above 40 per cent in 2008. However, 40 per cent of the jobs are still occupied by workers with education up to elementary school level or less (Table 2.3).

Table 2.2

Total Employment by Occupational Status and Net Growth during the Period 2003-2008

	2003		*2008*		*2003-2008*	
	Number	*%*	*Number*	*%*	*Number*	*%*
Registered wage-earners	29,264,358	33	38,069,128	38.9	8,804,770	95.5
Non-registered wage-earners	14,268,559	16.1	15,607,386	16	1,338,827	14.5
Self-employed	17,863,720	20.2	18,183,833	18.6	320,113	3.5
Domestic workers	6,147,143	6.9	6,568,765	6.7	421,622	4.6
Unpaid workers	5,642,387	6.4	4,258,549	4.4	-1,383,838	-15
Subsistence economy	3,400,905	3.8	3,946,310	4	545,405	5.9
Employers	3,359,867	3.8	4,096,075	4.2	736,208	8
Unemployed	8,637,122	9.8	7,070,432	7.2	-1,566,690	-17
Total	88,584,061	100	97,800,478	100	9,216,417	100

Source: PNAD/IBGE.

Table 2.3

Employment by Educational Level, 2003-08

	2003		*2008*	
	Number	*%*	*Number*	*%*
Elementary school or less	40,427,244	50.6	36,998,210	40.8
Incomplete high school	12,917,579	16.2	15,509,639	17.1
High school	19,856,736	24.8	28,797,403	31.7
Tertiary and more	6,218,952	7.8	9,040,906	10.0
Unknown	529,603	0.7	383,888	0.4
Total	79,950,114	100.0	90,730,046	100.0

Source: PNAD/IBGE.

These contrasting figures point to a very segmented labour market, one in which large groups of workers, even with improving access to education, cannot achieve better wages and social mobility.

On the other hand, it is striking that labour incomes fell more sharply for the more educated workers from 1998 up to 2003, and rose more slowly for the same group after 2003, as Figure 2.7 indicates. This has to do mainly with the large increase of the minimum wage in real terms, which may not continue in the long run. The problem of an 'over-educated labour force', at least in comparison to the low value-added jobs that have been created, may also explain this trend.

Figure 2.7

Index Numbers of Real Income from Work by Years of Schooling

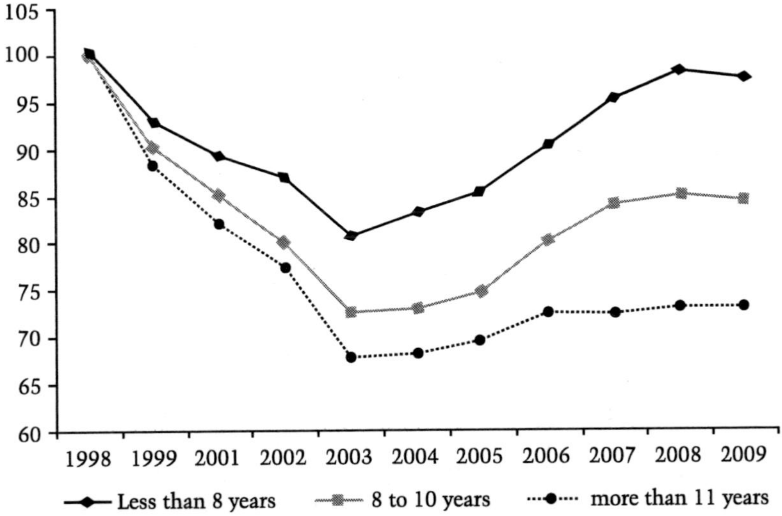

Source: PNAD/IBGE and IPEA.

Yet the wage gap is still large—around four times—between those with more than eleven years of schooling and those with less than eight years. Whether this gap will continue to decline depends on future trends in a number of factors: the continued reduction in the share of the labour force with less than eight years of schooling; the level of the minimum wage, acting as the reference price for the unskilled manual workforce, and pegged to GDP per capita; and the expansion of activities with high levels of productivity and value-added, which can pay higher wages to better qualified and educated workers.

In order to face the challenge of high inequality in the labour market, investment rates and productivity levels need to rise, accompanied by national level bargaining between labour and capital over the share of labour in total income. At the same time, pension, labour and trade union reforms should aim to broaden worker participation and extend the social security and labour code to those who are presently excluded from it. Moreover, as will be discussed in the following sections, cash transfer policies should be linked to public employment services, and universal social policies should be strengthened. Such a broad approach will only be feasible with an increasingly dynamic economy, built around intermediate and high-technology sectors and able to export a diversified basket of goods, and not only commodities.

To sum up, for the lower-income population, the tenure of the Lula Government was a period of rising employment, substantial wage and income gains, and social mobility. What is more, this was one of the few democratic periods in Brazil's history when the economy grew and income distribution improved, even if the development pattern did not change substantially.

This is underlined by a survey published by IPEA, the Institute of Applied Economic Research (Pochmann and Amorim, 2009), which shows a substantial upward movement of Brazilian households in economic terms between 2001 and 2007. In the survey, it was found that when the population was divided into three equal groups in terms of income in 2001, 10 million people, net, had moved from the lower-income group to the intermediate group by 2007. Moreover, another 3.8 million moved from the intermediate income group to the highest; that is, some 14 million people moved up across income thresholds, and the period when this occurred coincided with the recent years of economic growth and more active interventions by the State to fight poverty.

Nevertheless, the main features of a very unequal pattern of development remain, especially in the labour market structure. The upward movement was facilitated by the fact that the year 2003 was a low point in terms of income and employment levels, and in the subsequent recovery the dynamic internal market was able to assimilate workers who had been expelled in the 1990s. For these positive outcomes to continue in the future, a more substantial change in the development pattern is needed.

Brazil, like the other large BRICS countries, has an important asset in its internal market, which could be stimulated further through domestic investment, expansion of credit, and personal consumption. Although there are certainly sectors where it cannot compete with China and other players in the global market, the internal market provides the space to develop new sectors and productive chains. It would be essential to take advantage of this asset, if Brazil is not to experience the de-industrialization of its economy like its Latin American neighbours.

Finding its own development pattern in the global economy is fundamental for a change in the labour market structure and for a new set of social policies. This is a precondition if the country wants to leave behind its variety of dynamic and unequal 'dependent capitalism'.

Poverty and Inequality under the Lula Government

One of the highlights of the last decade was the reduction of poverty and social inequality in Brazil, which has been documented by several studies.[3] Moreover, this reduction, unprecedented for the country, is at the centre of the national agenda to such an extent that President Dilma Rousseff,[4] who succeeded President Lula, set as her administration's goal the eradication of extreme poverty.

However, the consensus among Brazilian analysts ends right there. What is the role of economic growth and of labour market dynamics and structure in shaping such a setting? What is the importance of raising the minimum wage and expanding social policies? How have employment, poverty and inequality interacted in the new macroeconomic context? And, more importantly, is it possible to sustain this virtuous circle without implementing new social inclusion policies, and coupling them with a model of economic growth that is less dependent on exogenous factors?

In this section and the next, we seek to show how poverty and inequality indicators have evolved in Brazil, and then present an overview of the new social policies that have been put into place, focusing specifically on cash transfer actions for the poorer segments of the population. The purpose is to discuss the role of these policies in improving the living conditions of these social strata, by presenting breakthroughs and indicating challenges that must be faced if, during the second decade of the twenty-first century, Brazil is to continue reducing poverty and inequality.

It is worth underlining the specificity of the Brazilian case compared with the other economies that make up the capitalist periphery. Brazil, despite its lower economic growth rates when compared to China, India and even South Africa, stands out for the dynamism of its labour market, which has stepped up the generation of formal employment, as we have seen above, while simultaneously reducing poverty and inequality, as we shall see below. Yet inequality is still considerably higher in Brazil than in China and India. Another difference is that the Brazilian poverty profile has become increasingly urban, in contrast to the situations in China and India. In the comparison with South Africa, what should be stressed is Brazil's capacity to raise employment levels and to reduce the informality rate, though the latter remains much higher than is found in developed countries.

In order to assess the evolution of poverty in Brazil, we used a poverty line set at ½ (half) the minimum wage per capita in the household. Between 1995 and 2007, the percentage of the population below this poverty line fell significantly (Figure 2.8). The downward trend was, however, not regular, as poverty changed little between 1995[5] and 2000, when it started declining, and more dramatically so as from 2004.

Figure 2.8 shows that the downward trend in poverty is similar for both black and non-black populations. Nonetheless, the proportion of poor people among the black population remains twice as high as among the non-black

Figure 2.8

Percentage of People Below the Poverty Line, by Race/Colour, 1995 to 2007 (Poverty Line= ½ Minimum Wage Per Capita)

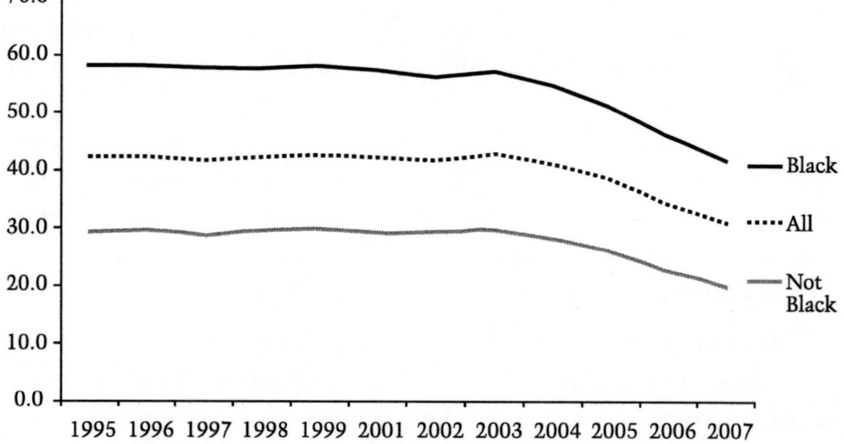

Source: IBGE, PNAD microdata. Graphics by IPEA, 2009.

population. Even though poverty has been reduced for the population as a whole, the gap between these two groups has hardly changed, underscoring the need for policies and instruments tailored to the black population if the race/colour divide is to be eliminated.

The decline in the percentage of the population classified as poor does not necessarily translate into a substantial gain in the quality of life of those who have risen above the poverty threshold, nor does it imply that access to social goods such as education, healthcare and housing, has increased. But there has clearly been a significant improvement in living conditions and in access to goods and services among the poor, not only because of the larger number of people with incomes exceeding half the minimum wage, but also because the minimum wage has itself increased by more than inflation over the period (by approximately 66 per cent in real terms over the decade).

In Brazil, poverty has always co-existed with great social inequality. During the recent period, the improved quality of life of the poorest has been accompanied by a lower income gap. This fact in itself is worthy of note, since lower poverty levels have often been accompanied by unchanging or worsening inequality, as in the 1970s; in fact, there is no record in Brazil after 1930—when the economy began to be monetized—of these two indicators ever falling simultaneously.

Nonetheless, the reduction in inequality was less substantial than the decline in poverty, in that the former has remained at high levels, especially when compared with other developed or under-developed countries. The trend in the Gini coefficient of income distribution (Figure 2.9) can help us better understand the recent changes.

As can be seen, income inequality as measured by the Gini coefficient—using household per capita income—remained stable throughout the second half of the 1990s. In 2001 it began to fall, and by the late 2000s, it reached a level that was 90 per cent of its value in 1995. In other words, though inequality did indeed fall, it still left Brazil a very unequal society. Income inequality is further compounded by disparities of asset and wealth ownership, in particular, land and urban property ownership.

Figure 2.9

Gini Coefficient from 1995 to 2009

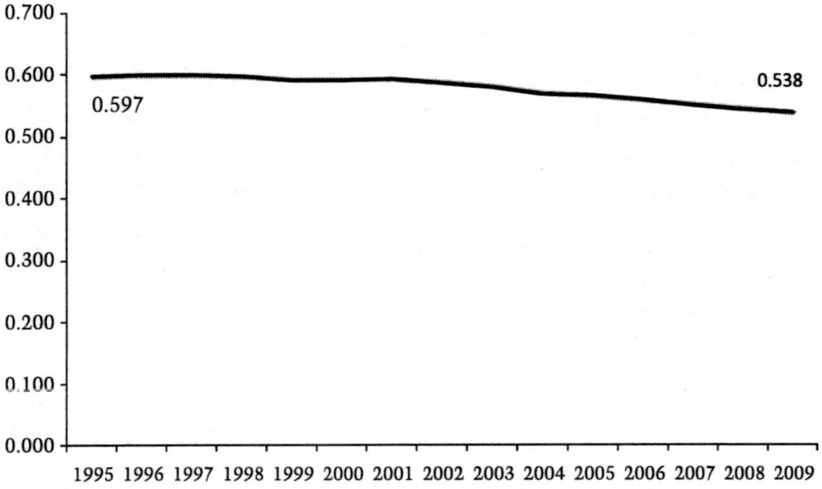

Source: IBGE, PNAD microdata. Graphics by IPEA, 2009.

The drop in inequality that started in 2001, and accelerated after 2004, can be at least partly explained by the recovery of the economy and growth in employment, which, as discussed earlier, brought into the formal labour market many workers who were previously unemployed or employed in low-income occupations, mostly in the informal sector. This process was further boosted by the recovery of the purchasing power of the minimum wage, which in 2009 had risen in real terms by two-thirds in comparison with the beginning of the decade, and by the expansion of social policies for the lower-income strata, which we discuss below.

It should be acknowledged, however, that half of the fall of the Gini coefficient occurred during the period 2004-2008, when it fell by 5 per cent, a substantial drop indeed, if we compare it to other periods in Brazilian history. The dynamism of the labour market, coupled with the social policies that we discuss in the next section, was strategic for this outcome, even though the impact varied across regions, states and within urban and rural areas, where we can find differing patterns of reproduction of inequality.

The increase of the minimum wage in real terms, together with increased employment (concentrated among those earning the lowest wages, close to minimum wage rates), also had an impact on another indicator of inequality. Figure 2.10 shows the functional distribution of value added between 2003 and 2008. The share of wages and salaries in national income rose by a little over 2 percentage points, from 39.3 to 41.9 per cent, while the share of profits fell from 45.9 to 41.9 per cent, and government revenues grew by slightly over 1 percentage point, reaching 16.2 per cent of national income in 2008.

Figure 2.10

Distribution of National Income, 2003-2008

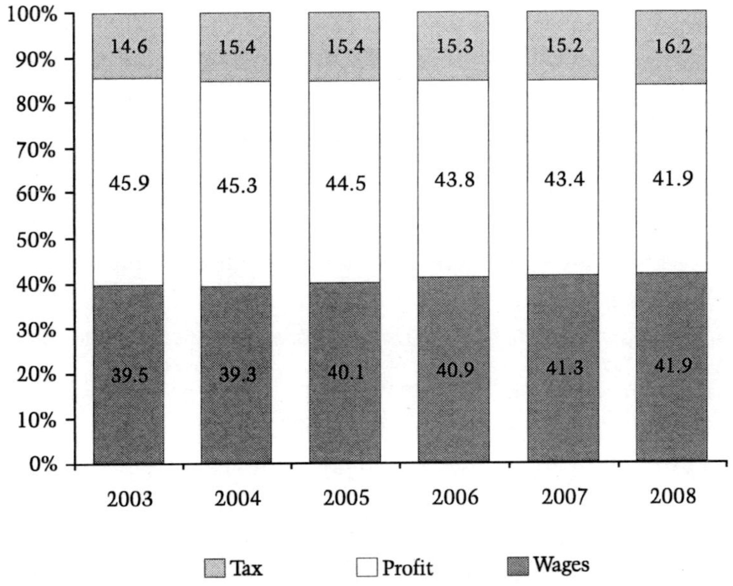

Note: Profit includes income of self-employed workers and individual employers.

Source: IBGE, Directorship of Research, Coordination of National Accounts. Graphics by the author.

Although this change was fairly small, it is significant that during the second half of the 2000s, the share of labour in national income did grow, albeit slowly (at 1.2 per cent a year), whereas the share of capital fell at an annual rate of 1.7 per cent (largely owing to a drop in the income of the self-employed). The decrease in the profit share occurred in the context of re-activated domestic demand, so there was nevertheless an increase in the absolute level of profits.

Summing up, we can say that throughout the 2000s, and especially in the second half of the decade, there was an improvement in social conditions, with a decrease in the proportion of the population below the poverty line and a reduction in income inequality, which was much faster during the period 2004-2008. This improvement was largely due to good economic performance, which generated a large number of formal jobs, absorbing both the growing working population and unemployed workers. Furthermore, a higher minimum wage, plus the extension of cash transfer policies to workers on the fringes of the labour market, had a positive impact on the income of those at the bottom of the pyramid. While huge income disparities persist, this increased income had an important effect on inequality, which could be seen in the reduction of the Gini coefficient.

Cash Transfer Policies and Social Exclusion in Brazil

Social protection in Brazil made great strides after the promulgation of the democratic Federal Constitution in 1988. New rights were won, especially access of rural workers to social security, while the ways and means to fund social policy were established, both critical factors in determining the broadened coverage and growth of social spending as from the 1990s.

The institutional framework ushered in by the new Federal Constitution made it possible to adopt a host of public social protection policies. These included unemployment insurance, which, though created in 1986, actually materialized with the introduction of the tax creating the Workers' Protection Fund (FAT) in 1990, which also regulated the funding of that insurance, as provided for in the Constitution. Since then, unemployment insurance has widened, covering 66 per cent to 75 per cent of all workers laid off without just cause every year (Moretto, 2009). Still, coverage for all unemployed workers does not exceed 20 per cent (Barbosa, 2007).

Non-contributory transfer programmes were devised to meet the needs of the poor. Among these is the Continuous Instalment Benefit (BPC), which provides assistance income for extremely poor elderly people (aged 65-plus) and disabled persons (belonging to households with per capita income of a quarter of a minimum wage).[6] The introduction of this benefit meant an increase in the coverage of the elderly in terms of protecting their income. The year it was implemented (1996) it catered to 346,000 beneficiaries, while in 2004 its coverage had increased to a total of 2.06 million beneficiaries (Vaitsman, *et al.*, 2009).

To give an idea of the recent evolution in the coverage of the BPC, Figure 2.11 shows the number of people benefiting from this public policy from 2004 to 2010. The total number of beneficiaries rises from 2.06 million in 2004 to 3.40 million in 2010, a 65 per cent increase. It should be underscored that the rise in the elderly population as a proportion of all BPC beneficiaries stems from the changing demographics in Brazil, with an increase in the population aged 65 or more. However, this transition alone does not account for the growing number of elderly people receiving the benefit. It is imperative to understand Brazil's labour market, in that its consolidation process was unable to protect the entire workforce—mainly those occupied in agricultural activities—through labour laws and social protection. Consequently, a substantial proportion of the elderly is eligible for the programme. The BPC aims to correct, in part, this social debt, which

Figure 2.11

Continuous Instalment Benefits: Total Number of People per Benefit, 2004 to 2010 (in thousands of people)

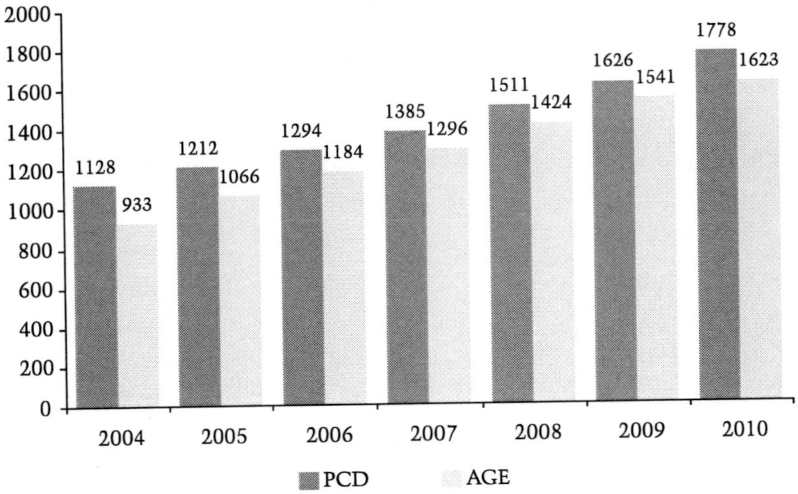

Note: PCD – disabled persons; AGE – elderly people.

Source: MDS/SAGI (Available at *http://aplicacoes.mds.gov.br/sagi/mi2007/tabelas/mi_social.php*, accessed July 10, 2011). Graph by the authors.

accounts for the upward trend that the programme has exhibited ever since it was created.

During the 1990s, many municipalities launched cash transfer programmes catering to low-income families on condition that their school-age children—up to 14 years of age—attended basic education programmes. These experiences influenced the introduction of such programmes at the national level. The first national programme to be implemented was the Programme for the Eradication of Child Labour (PETI), in 1996, which sought to reach out to 7-to-15-year-olds, keeping them at school and in extra-curricular activities all day long and away from working on the streets, in exchange for financial compensation to their families. In 2001, this programme was followed by the Federal School Grant Programme, the Food Allowance Programme and the Food Stamp Programme, all of which transferred cash to families upon fulfillment of one condition. In the case of the Federal School Grant, the families benefited had to keep their children at school, with a minimum attendance of 85 per cent throughout the year. The Food Allowance Programme required beneficiaries to attend pre-natal exams, and breastfeed and vaccinate their children. Finally, the Food Stamp Programme was aimed at low-income families, which had to spend the money exclusively on food (Soares and Satyro, 2010, p. 30).

Despite their positive aspects and importance for the population benefited, these programmes were not conceived in a context of coherent and strategic government action. Actions were not coordinated and programmes were implemented by different ministries: Ministry of Education (School Grant); Ministry of Health (Food Allowance, Food Stamp); Ministry of Mines and Energy (Cooking Gas Allowance)[7]; and Ministry of Labour and Employment (PETI).

The change of government, in 2003, paved the way for the reformulation of the conditional cash transfer policy, culminating in the Family Allowance Programme (PBF). The PBF is the responsibility of the National Department for Citizen's Income (Senarc) of the Ministry for Social Development and Fight against Hunger, which is responsible for social assistance and food and nutritional security policies. The Senarc is responsible for implementing the national policy for citizen's income and for managing the PBF jointly with the states, the Federal District and the municipalities. Besides, the Senarc also manages the Single Registry, the database for all social programmes.

In line with the decentralized managerial model adopted, municipalities are responsible for registering the poor families, whose data are collected through a questionnaire prepared by Senarc and fed into the Single Registry database. In addition, municipalities are responsible for preparing the follow-up reports regarding the requirements that are to be met by beneficiaries.

Still regarding PBF operational aspects, the role of the State-owned bank Caixa Econômica Federal must be underscored, as this institution operates and disburses all benefits, besides processing the information held in the Single Registry, all in accordance with Senarc guidelines.

The PBF is intended for poor families, that is, whose per capita income is below the poverty line (per capita income below R$140 per month, or US$82). These families are divided into two groups on the basis of an extreme poverty line (income per head lower than R$70). The amount paid out monthly in the form of benefit to each family (the figures are for February 2011) ranges from R$22.00 (US$13) to R$200.00 (US$118),

Box 2.1

The Structure of the Family Allowance (PBF)

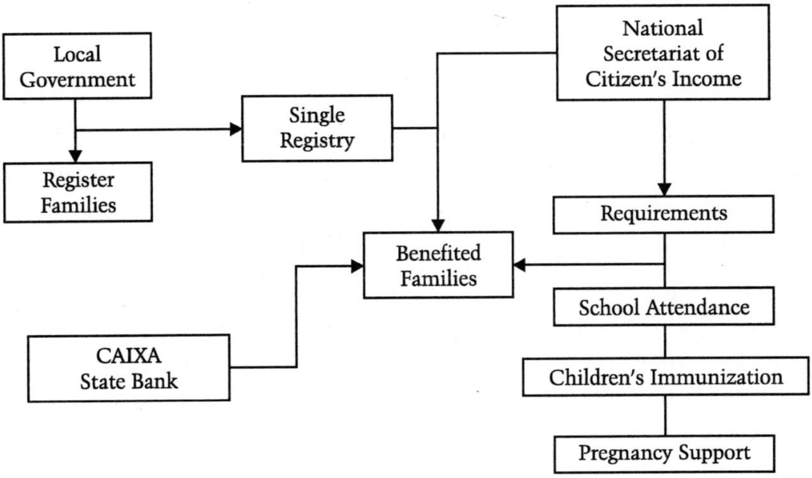

depending on the type of benefit and how poor the family is, as measured by per capita income. The four types of benefits offered are as follows:

(i) Basic: Amounting to R$68.00 (US$40), the benefit is paid to every family classified as in extreme poverty regardless of the number of children and teenagers in the family.

(ii) Variable: Amounting to R$22.00 (US$13), the benefit is paid to every poor or extremely poor family with children aged up to 15, limited to three children per family. Hence, the highest amount paid is R$66.00 per family.

(iii) Variable and Teenager: Amounting to R$33.00 (US$19), the benefit is paid to every family with teenagers in the 16-17 age range. Top payment for each family is R$66.00, that is, a maximum of two teenagers in this age range.

(iv) Variable and of an Extraordinary Nature: With no fixed amount, the benefit is paid to every family migrating from any of the earlier programmes (Cooking Gas, School Grant, Food Allowance, and Food Stamp) to the Family Allowance Programme.

The total amount received by a family is the sum of the various benefits, depending upon the characteristics of the family concerned. The basic difference between a poor family and an extremely poor family is that the latter receives both the basic benefit (even those families that consist of adults only) and the applicable variable benefits. Poor families only receive variable benefits and, in this case, families whose members are all aged 18 or more are not entitled to benefits.

The PBF is not a 'right'. The fact that the characteristics of a family would make it eligible for the programme does not necessarily mean that this family would become a beneficiary. The reason for this can be found in the programme's funding arrangements, as the programme's budget is defined by the Government on a yearly basis. Thus, the number of families benefited by the programme is not necessarily the same as the number of families that are eligible to enter the programme (Soares and Satyro, 2010). Nevertheless, the number of families benefiting from the programme has grown substantially, from 6.57 million families in 2004 to 12.78 million in 2010 (Figure 2.12).

Figure 2.12

Families Benefiting from the Family Allowance Programme, 2004-2010 (in millions)

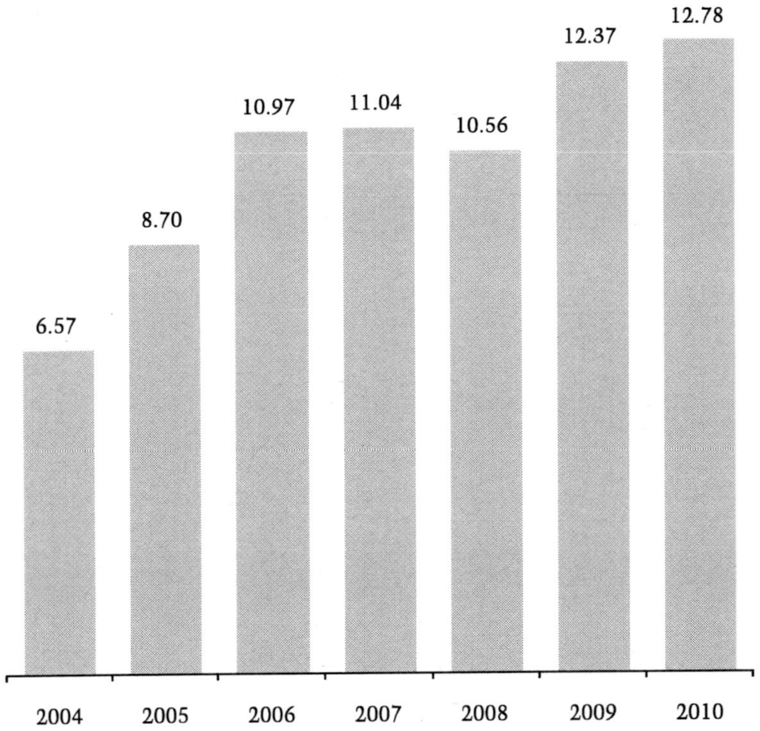

Notes: (i) In millions of families; (ii) Data for 2010 refer to November.

Source: MDS/SAGI (Available at : *http://aplicacoes.mds.gov.br/sagi/mi2007/tabelas/mi_social.php*, accessed July 10, 2011). Graph prepared by authors.

Expenditures on all cash transfer programmes combined (Figure 2.13) rose from slightly less than 7 per cent of GDP to 9 per cent of GDP between 2002 and 2009. Although the funds earmarked for the PBF doubled—from 0.19 per cent to 0.39 per cent in 2009—this programme accounts for only a small fraction of the total. Among the other programmes, the BPC (the social assistance benefit) pays one minimum wage to people aged 65 and over, and special needs persons in extremely poor families. If we consider that between 2003 and 2010, the minimum wage grew by approximately 56 per cent in real terms, we can see the magnitude of the income increase for the beneficiaries of this programme. Also, in the case of unemployment insurance and retirement benefits and pensions, the lowest value paid is the minimum wage, with a great concentration of beneficiaries getting this amount.

Figure 2.13

Expenditures on Cash Transfer Programmes, 2002-2009 (in per cent of GDP)

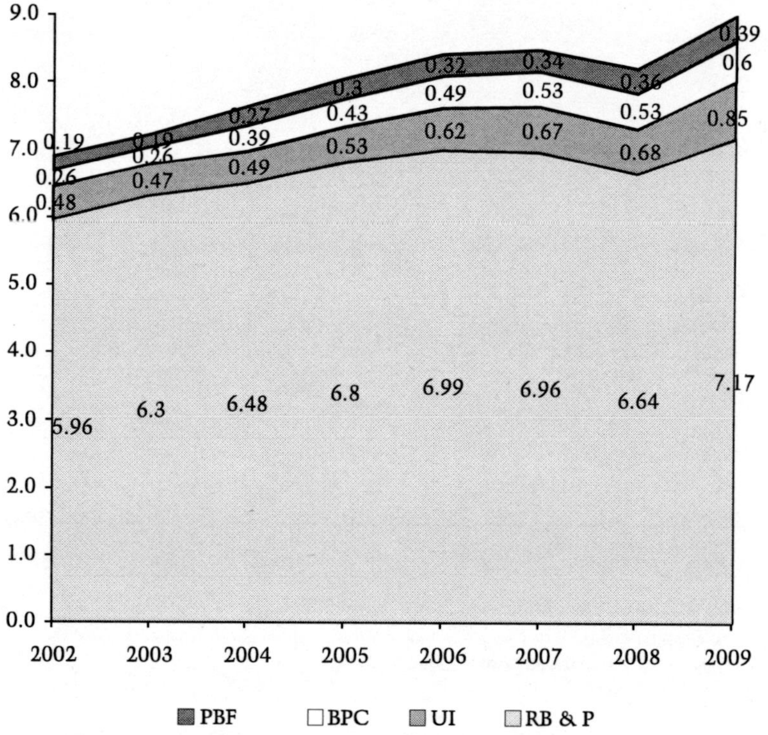

Notes: (i) UI = unemployment insurance; (ii) RB&P = retirement benefits and pensions (does not include public employees).

Source: Ministry of the Economy, SPE, in Barbosa and Souza, 2010, p. 37.

The expansion of cash transfer programmes targeting the poorest, such as the Family Allowance and the Continuous Instalment Benefit, plus other State and local programmes, has changed the pattern of household income for families which benefit from these programmes. There has been a significant increase in income classified as 'other sources' to the detriment of income from labour and from social security and pensions.

Table 2.4 shows that for the set of all families, revenues from 'other sources' accounted for 5.0 per cent of a household's total income in 2009, income earned from work 76.2 per cent, and retirement and pensions 18.8 per cent. In extremely poor families (with a family income per capita of up to a quarter of a minimum wage), income from 'other sources' represented 28.0 per cent of total family income in 2009, with retirement accounting for 5.8 per cent, and work-related income for two-thirds of the total (IBGE, 2010).

Table 2.4

Sources of Income of Poor and Extremely Poor Families, 2009 (in per cent of total income)

Family Type	*Source of Income*		
	Labour	*Retirement and Pensions*	*Other*
Total	76.2	18.8	5.0
Poor	75.2	14.0	10.7
Extremely Poor	66.2	5.8	28.0

Source: IBGE, 2010.

The impact of cash transfer programmes, including retirement payments for rural workers, can be better assessed when we look at changes in the share of families classified as 'poor' and as 'extremely poor' between 1995 and 2008, as shown in Table 2.5. Both fell sharply, and extreme poverty was halved.

Table 2.5

Poor and Extremely Poor Families, 1995 and 2008 (per cent of total population)

Income per capita	*1995*	*2008*
≤ ½ Minimum Wage	43.4	28.8
≤ ¼ Minimum Wage	20.9	10.5

Source: IPEA, 2010a. Table prepared by the authors.

In addition to the impact on the living conditions of the families benefiting from conditional cash transfers, these programmes can sustain—provided they are coupled with other policies—a growth policy hinged on the expansion of the domestic market and of aggregate demand. Hence, cash transfer programmes, together with a policy designed to increase the minimum wage, along with the expansion of consumer credit, have fuelled the recent growth cycle (Barbosa and Souza, 2010).

Yet long-term sustained growth is bound to depend on raising investment levels and lowering import dependence, with increased internalization of productivity gains and increased tax collection by the State. This scenario could lead to wage increases—via sector-wide collective bargaining—so that a growing share of wages in national income would become less dependent on minimum wage raises. At the same time, in the medium term, further reductions in poverty and inequality are likely to rely less on cash transfer policies—for a good part of the families have already benefited—and more on policies in other fields: structural reforms of employment and vocational training policies, policies designed to increase access to healthcare and education (and improving the quality of these services), and a tax reform that reduces the taxes levied on lower-income groups.

Concluding Remarks

We hope to have given some clues to answer the question posed in the title of the paper: What changed in the Lula Government? Brazil managed, in a short period—which included a tough international financial crisis—to resume growth, while at the same time delivering positive results in terms of employment and labour incomes, especially for disadvantaged groups. Moreover, the expansion of cash transfer policies clearly contributed to the reduction of poverty. All these factors taken together led to some reduction in income inequality, though it still remains high by international standards. And the internal market worked once again as an engine of growth.

On the other hand, it is not clear whether Brazil has moved decisively away from its earlier variety of capitalism, which coupled economic dynamism and social inequality, a heterogeneous labour market and the inability to universalize access to social policies. Moreover, the dynamism of the internal market is concentrated in sectors that are not known for their high value-added and productivity levels. This may, in the future, hamper the country's capacity for raising the level and share of wages in national income and for increasing social expenditures, and be a renewed source of external vulnerability. This is what has not changed in the Lula Government, posing new challenges for the coming years, if Brazil is to maintain its good performance in terms of labour market outcomes, while continuing to reduce levels of poverty and inequality.

References

Amable, B. (2005). *Les cinq capitalismes: Diversités des systèmes économiques et sociaux dans la mondialisation*. Paris: Éditions du Seuil.

Barbosa, A.F. (2003). *A formação do mercado de trabalho no Brasil*. São Paulo: Editorial Alameda.

———. (2007). "O seguro-desemprego, o mercado de trabalho e o sistema público de emprego, trabalho e renda", in *A qualificação profissional e o sistema público de emprego, trabalho e renda*, São Paulo: DIEESE/MTE.

Barbosa, Nelson and José Antonio Pereira de Souza (2010). "A inflexão do governo Lula: Política econômica, crescimento e distribuição de renda", in Emir Sader and Marco Aurélio Garcia (eds), *Brasil: Entre o passado e o futuro*. São Paulo: Boitempo.

Barros, Ricardo P. De, Mirela de Carvalho, Samuel Franco and Rosane Mendonça (2007). *A queda recente da desigualdade de renda no Brasil*. Texto para Discussao n.1258. IPEA. January. Rio de Janeiro.

Belluzzo, L.G. and J.G. Almeida (2002). *Depois da queda: A economia Brasileira da crise da dívida aos impasses do Real*. Rio de Janeiro: Civilização Brasileira.

Boyer, R. and J.R. Hollingsworth (1997). "From National Embeddedness to Spatial and Institutional Nestedness", in R. Boyer and J.R. Hollingsworth (eds), *Contemporary Capitalism: The Embeddedness of Institutions*. Cambridge: Cambridge University Press.

Cacciamali, Maria C. and Vladimir S. Camillo (2009). "Redução da desigualdade da distribuição de renda entre 2001 e 2006 nas macrorregiões brasileiras: Tendência ou fenômeno transitório?", *Economia e Sociedade* 18(2): 287-316.

Cardoso, F.H. and E. Faletto (1970). *Dependência e desenvolvimento na América Latina: Ensaio de interpretação sociológica*. Rio de Janeiro: Guanabara. 7th edition.

Evans, P. (1979). *Dependent Development: The Alliance of Multinational, State and Local Capital in Brazil*. Princeton: Princeton University Press.

Fernandes, F. (1987). *A revolução burguesa no Brasil*. Rio de Janeiro: Editora Guanabara. 3rd edition.

Franco, G. (1999). *O desafio Brasileiro: Ensaios sobre desenvolvimento, globalização e moeda*. São Paulo: Editora 34.

Furtado, C. (1965). *Desenvolvimento e subdesenvolvimento*. Rio de Janeiro: Fundo de Cultura. 3rd edition.

———. (1974). *O mito do desenvolvimento econômico*. São Paulo: Paz e Terra. 4th edition.

Gray, J. (1998). *False Dawn: Delusions of Global Capitalism*. New York: New Press.

Instituto Brasileiro de Geografia e Estatística (IBGE) (2010). *Síntese de Indicadores Sociais: Uma Análise das Condições de Vida da População Brasileira*, Estudos e Pesquisas. Informação Demográfica e Socioeconômica. No.27. Rio de Janeiro.

Instituto de Pesquisas Econômicas Aplicadas (IPEA) (2009). *Políticas Sociais: Acompanhamento e análise—Vinte Anos da Constituição Federal*. No.17 (Statistical Annex). Brasília.

———. (2010a). *Dimensão, evolução e projeção da pobreza por região e por estado no Brasil*. Comunicado do IPEA. No. 58. Brasília. July.

———. (2010b). *PNAD 2009 – primeiras analises: distribuição de renda entre 1995 e 2009*, Comunicado do IPEA. No. 63. Brasília. October.

Jakobsen, K. and A.F. Barbosa (2008). "Neo-liberal Policies, Labour Market Restructuring and Social Exclusion: Brazil's Working Class Response", in A. Bieler, I. Lindberg and D. Pillay (eds), *Labour and the Challenges of Globalization: What Prospects for Transnational Solidarity?* London: Pluto Press.

Kupfer, D. (2005). "Tecnologia e emprego são realmente antagônicos", in J. Sicsú, L.F. de Paula and R. Michel (eds), *Novo-desenvolvimentistmo: Um projeto nacional de crescimento com eqüidade social*. Rio de Janeiro: Manole.

Leone, Eugenia T., Alexandre G. Maia and Paulo Baltar (2010). "Mudanças na composição das famílias e impactos sobre a redução da pobreza no Brasil", *Economia e Sociedade* 19(1): 59-78.

Moretto, Amilton (2009). *O sistema público de emprego, trabalho e renda: Uma construção inacabada*. Coleção Debates Contemporâneos. No. 6. São Paulo: LTr.

Oliveira, F. (2003). *Crítica à razão dualista*. São Paulo: Editorials Boitempo.

Pochmann, M. (1998). *O trabalho sob fogo cruzado*. São Paulo: Editora Contexto.

Pochmann, M. and R.L.C. Amorim (2009). "Pobreza e mudanças sociais recentes no Brasil", in Jorge Abrahão de Castro and José Aparecido Carlos Ribeiro (eds), *Situação social brasileira: 2007*. Brasília: IPEA.

Prebisch, R. (1981). *Capitalismo periférico: Crisis y transformación*. México: Fondo de Cultura Económica.

Rocha, S. (2004). *Pobreza no Brasil: Afinal do que se trata?*. Rio de Janeiro: Editora FGV.

Santos, J.A.F. (2002). *Estrutura de posições de classe no Brasil*. Rio de Janeiro: IUPERJ.

Serrano, Franklin and Ricardo Summa (2011). *Política macroeconômica, crescimento e distribuição de renda na economia brasileira dos anos 2000*. Observatório da Economia Global No. 6. IE/Unicamp, Centro de Estudos de Conjuntura e política econômica. Campinas, March. Available at *http://www.iececon.net/arquivos/OBSERVATORIO_6.pdf*, accessed on 15 March 2011.

Soares, Sergei and Natália Sátyro (2010). "O programa Bolsa Família: Desenho institucional e possibilidades futuras", in Jorge A. De Castro and Lúcia Modesto (eds), *Bolsa Família 2003-2010: Avanços e desafios*. Vol.1. pp.27-56. Brasília: IPEA.

Vaitsman, Jeni, Gabriela R.B. de Andrade and Luís O. Farias (2009). "Proteção social no Brasil: o que mudou na assistência social após a Constituição de 1988" in *Ciência and Saúde Coletiva* 14(3): 731-41. Rio de Janeiro.

Notes

1. The concept of under-development has been extensively criticized to the point of being devalued academically. However, it should be stressed that this concept is more workable than its variants such as emerging, developing and newly industrializing economies. By under-developed countries, we mean those societies that were a by-product of the expansion of European capitalism, without reproducing all of its dynamics and institutions. They evolve according to the changes of global capitalism, but have their own internal dynamics. In our view, the so-called 'theory of under-development' and 'dependency theory' should be seen not as closed theories, distinct

from the social sciences tradition developed in the West, but as a framework for historical analysis in a concrete and very specific set of economic and social structures.

2. The official inflation rate would subsequently only be close to or higher than two digits in moments of strong currency devaluation, as in 1999 to 2002.
3. For example, Barros *et al.* (2007); Cacciamali and Camilo (2009); Leone *et al.* (2010); IPEA (2010b).
4. Dilma Rousseff was sworn in on 1 January 2011 to succeed President Luiz Inácio Lula da Silva. The incumbent president was Minister of Mines and Energy and, later on, Chief of Staff during the Lula administration.
5. 1995, as a result of the stabilization of the economy, poverty levels were already much lower than in 1993.
6. The minimum wage approved for 2011 is worth R$545.00 (approximately US$ 320.59 at an exchange rate of R$1.70 to US$1.00). Further amounts denominated in dollars in the text are based on this rate.
7. The Vale-Gás (cooking gas allowance programme) was created in 2003 to compensate for the elimination of a subsidy on cooking gas. It targeted low-income families and set no conditionality.

3 Labour Markets and Social Protection in China

Experiences and Issues

Du Yang

Recent Developments in the Chinese Labour Market

With fast economic growth in the past decades, China has also witnessed substantial labour market development through the introduction of market mechanisms in labour allocation, reform of the social protection system, and improved regulations. Developments in the Chinese labour market reflect both labour mobility driven by labour market signals and institutional changes guided by labour market policies. In detail, recent labour market developments in China could be summarized as follows.

During the early reform period—that is, from the early 1980s through the mid-1990s—employment in rural and urban China expanded mainly through the transformation of farmers into non-agricultural workers. Job creation by township and village enterprises and massive labour migration from rural to urban sectors underpinned the impressive, unique and worldwide-recognized 'China miracle'.

Since the 1990s, rural to urban migration has played a dominant role in labour mobility. In 2010, migrant workers[1] from rural areas totalled 153 million, and they have become an indispensable component in the urban labour market. Since rural-to-urban migration was driven by large-scale surplus labour in rural areas, it generates two effects of transition and development. The first is the effect of resource re-allocation, namely, labour transfer from sectors with low productivity (agriculture) to those with high productivity (secondary and tertiary sectors). This alone contributed 21 per cent to the overall GDP growth rate during the early reform period (Cai and Wang, 1999), and 16.7 per cent during the past decade (Cai, *et al.*, 2010). The second one is the income effect—that is, while the wage rate of migrant workers is lower than that of urban workers with local *hukou* (household registration) on average, because of remittances, the increase in the total number of migrants has enhanced the income of rural households as a whole.

The planned economy was characterized by a rigid employment system in firms. Prior to the reform, the State Owned Enterprises (SOEs) seldom had rights to make hiring or firing decisions. In the middle of the 1980s, the Chinese Government began to relax the restrictions on SOEs and gave more rights to the enterprises, including the right to take some employment decisions. More significant reforms were introduced in the 1990s when SOEs abandoned full employment protection for their employees. This reform is called shattering the iron-rice bowl, and it introduced market mechanisms into the urban economy, in particular in the SOEs. Reforming the employment system of SOEs made the Chinese labour market more competitive than before.

Meanwhile, those who were laid off and the unemployed started to seek jobs in informal sectors, which led to informalization of the urban labour market. In order to cope with the disadvantages of informalization, social safety nets that were compatible with the market economy were set up.

A rapid demographic transition and fast economic growth have between them driven the Chinese labour market through the Lewis turning point where the unlimited labour supply ended. Accompanying increasing total employment, shortage of unskilled workers appeared first in China's fast growing regions where industry has been dominated by labour-intensive sectors, and the shortage then spread to other parts of China. In recent years, labour shortage has been more widespread and the wages of unskilled workers have been rising; it is this that shows most clearly that China has passed through the Lewis turning point.

The implications of passing the turning point are substantial, and the most obvious one is that workers who previously had weak bargaining power in the labour market now have more choices by voting with their feet. Since the demographic transition has been one of the most important driving forces that caused labour shortage, it is reasonable to believe that the phenomenon is the beginning of a long-term trend rather than a temporary one.

If we see rural-to-urban migration and urban economic restructuring as relaxing control over labour allocation, the improvement of the legal framework in recent years assumes increasing importance as a procedure to regulate the labour market. Passing the Lewis turning point implies that there is a possibility of building a more regulated labour market without losing competitiveness if the trade-off between flexibility and security is finely chosen. A number of labour-related laws have been enacted in recent years. Meanwhile, China is also beginning to seek a suitable point in the labour market that achieves both flexibility and security.

Economic Growth and Employment Creation in China

It is well known that China has experienced remarkable economic growth during the past three decades. Although economic growth in China has been subject to fluctuations when outside shocks occurred, for example, the Asian financial crisis in the 1990s and the recent global financial crisis, China has been one of the economies with the highest economic growth rates in the world since 1990. Since 1978, when China began to implement the strategy of opening up and reforms, the average growth rate of real GDP has been 11 per cent per annum at 1978 prices.

In the new century, China continues its striking economic performance even after maintaining high growth rates for a quarter of a century. It only took China five years to increase its GDP per capita from USD 1,000 to USD 2,000 at current prices, though that is partly due to the appreciation of the renmimbi with respect to the US dollar. Despite being hit by the recent global financial crisis, the GDP growth rate still reached 9 per cent in 2008, and more than 10 per cent in 2009 and 2010. In 2010, China's GDP was 39,798 billion yuan and GDP per capita reached 29,748 yuan, equivalent to USD 6,021 billion and USD 4,500, respectively.

Accompanying the fast economic growth, a substantial sectoral shift has taken place during the past decades. There are two features of this sectoral shift that are worth noting here, which, in turn, have affected labour market outcomes significantly.

First, as a developing economy, China follows the typical growth pattern of a shrinking primary sector. Figure 3.1 depicts the general trend of economic transformation in which the share of the primary sector in GDP keeps declining. In 1990, the value added of the primary sector[2] accounted for about 27.1 per cent of total GDP, falling to 10.6 per cent in 2009. In contrast to the primary sector, non-agricultural sectors have progressively increased their shares in the Chinese economy. For instance, the value added of the tertiary sector, which accounted for 31.6 per cent of GDP in 1990, went up to 42.4 per cent in 2009.

Figure 3.1

GDP Composition in China, 1990-2007

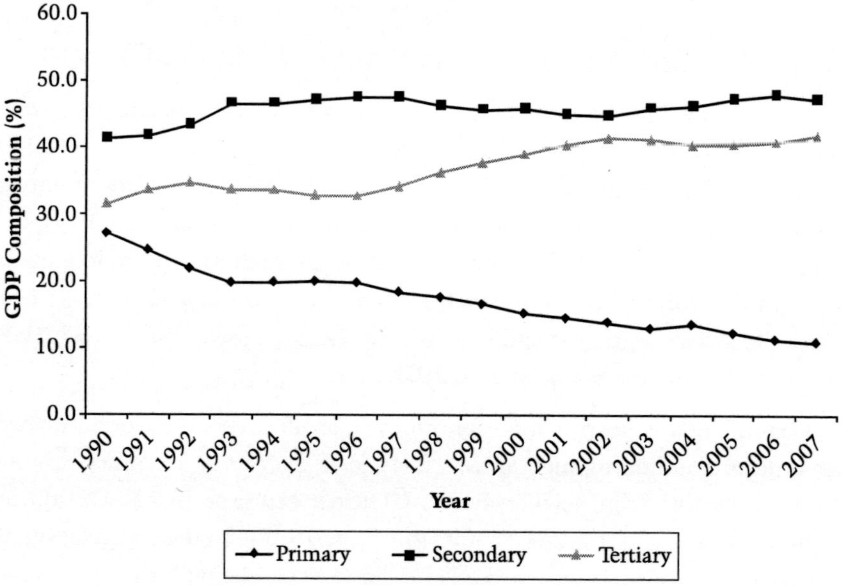

Source: NBS, Statistical Yearbook of 2008, China Statistical Press.

Second, the manufacturing sectors have maintained a stable proportion in the economy, which is a unique pattern for an economy undergoing economic restructuring. During the process of economic transformation in the developed economies, the expansion of the tertiary sector took place alongside a simultaneous shrinking of the secondary sector. Data from the World Bank Development Indicators show that even the lower-middle income countries today already display such a trend. This is not yet the case in China. In line with the Flying Geese Model, the coastal areas started accepting the industries transferred from the New Industrialized

Economies (NIEs) in the mid-1980s. Since then, China has made good use of its competitive advantages in labour-intensive industries. As a result, the share of the secondary sector in GDP has been stable since 1978, fluctuating around 45 per cent with a small standard deviation of 2.02 percentage points.

China has taken advantage of its abundant labour after entry into the World Trade Organization (WTO) and has become the 'factory of the world', as evidenced by the dominant role of the label 'Made in China' in international trade. In 2009, the ratio of the total value of exports to GDP was 0.37, as compared with a ratio of 0.20 in 2001 when China had just entered the WTO.

The growth pattern is also reflected in the labour market outcomes. First, fast economic growth has created job opportunities and has sustained the growth of total employment in China. Second, the economic shift from agriculture to non-agricultural sectors also leads to an employment shift among economic sectors, and, in turn, causes the large flow of rural-to-urban migration. Third, the booming export-oriented sectors created a large number of job vacancies. As evidenced by recent labour market changes, the greater integration with other economies also increased employment instability through both changes in labour demand and external shocks.

Table 3.1 presents the major labour market outcomes in the Chinese case. Although a recent study (Du and Wang, 2011), which drew on various sources of information, indicates an over-estimation in total employment, the following statistics show the trend of increasing total employment. Urban economic restructuring caused significant labour market shocks in the 1990s, but thanks to fast economic growth after the crisis, total employment has kept increasing during the past decade, as shown in Table 3.1. Also, China has quickly recovered from the recent global financial crisis, as can be seen from the growth of total employment.

The labour force participation and unemployment rates reported in China do not follow the standard international definitions proposed by the ILO. Registered unemployment is defined as the number of registered unemployed persons in urban areas with non-agricultural household registration aged 16 years and above who are capable of working, unemployed and willing to work, and have been registered at local employment service agencies to apply for jobs. Under such a definition, work status and willingness to work are not the only conditions for unemployment definitions, since *hukou* status and registration for unemployment are also indispensable factors. As we may see in the table, there are only small fluctuations in registered unemployment rates, which implies that this indicator is not an ideal one to measure the labour market situation in China.

Table 3.1

Total Employment, Labour Force Participation, and Unemployment in China

Year	*Economically Active Population (million)*	*Total Employment (million)*	*Urban Labour Market*			
			Employment (million)	*LFP (%)*	*UR (%)*	*RUR (%)*
1990	653.23	647.49	170.41	78.0	3.26	2.5
1991	660.91	654.91	174.65	83.0	3.32	2.3
1992	667.82	661.52	178.61	72.6	3.41	2.3
1993	674.68	668.08	182.62	66.9	3.49	2.6
1994	681.35	674.55	186.53	72.3	3.52	2.8
1995	688.55	680.65	190.40	75.9	3.98	2.9
1996	697.65	689.50	199.22	72.9	3.93	3.0
1997	708.00	698.20	207.81	72.1	4.50	3.1
1998	720.87	706.37	216.16	71.2	6.29	3.1
1999	727.91	713.94	224.12	72.9	5.87	3.1
2000	739.92	720.85	231.51	66.1	7.61	3.1
2001	744.32	730.25	239.40	67.3	5.55	3.6
2002	753.60	737.40	247.80	66.5	6.14	4.0
2003	760.75	744.32	256.39	63.4	6.02	4.3
2004	768.23	752.00	264.76	64.0	5.78	4.2
2005	778.77	758.25	273.31	62.5	5.80	4.2
2006	782.44	764.00	283.10	63.6	6.12	4.1
2007	786.45	769.90	293.50	63.0	5.34	4.0
2008	794.23	774.80	302.10	62.6		4.2
2009	798.12	779.95	311.20	62.4		4.3

Note: LFP: Labour Force Participation, UR: Unemployment Rate, RUR: Registered Unemployment Rate.
Source: NBS, China Statistical Yearbook (various years), China Statistical Press.

Alternatively, with some assumptions, it is possible to estimate a survey-based urban unemployment rate on the basis of various sources of data published by the National Bureau of Statistics (NBS). Both survey-based unemployment rates and registered unemployment rates are shown in Table 3.1. It can be seen that the registered unemployment rate underestimates the actual unemployment situation in the urban labour market: the surveyed unemployment rate is always higher than the registered unemployment rate. The gap between the two rates has been more substantial since the middle of 1990s when the urban labour market witnessed a significant dislocation. The declining unemployment rate since the turn of the century reflects the improved labour market situation in recent years.

China has been transformed from a dual economy into an industrialized country and also shows the widespread trend of a declining primary sector. Accompanied by the economic restructuring already described above, secondary and tertiary activities have become the dominant economic sectors providing job vacancies in China. Again, official employment statistics may bias the reported employment structure, but the trends of structural changes in employment are plausible. As Figure 3.2 shows, employment in the primary sector accounted for a decreasing proportion of total employment. In 1990, 60 per cent of the total labour force worked in agriculture while the share dropped to 41 per cent in 2007. China's comparative advantage in labour-intensive industry and the opportunities created by globalization made it possible for the country to take advantage of its rich human resources. Unlike other economies, China has kept its share of manufacturing at a stable level. In 1997, employment in the secondary sector accounted for 23.7 per cent of total employment, increasing to 27.8 per cent in 2009. This trend resulted in a significant migration flow within China.

China has witnessed the largest labour migration in the world since the reform and opening up policies were implemented. According to the most recent statistics, the total number of rural-to-urban migrant workers has been increasing during the past decades, as Figure 3.3 depicts. The migration flow has propelled the economic and societal transition in China through the increase of labour productivity and social restructuring. Accordingly, the Chinese Government has adapted its migration policies to take into account increasing migration flow and changes in the labour market.

Figure 3.2

Employment by Economic Sector, 1990-2007

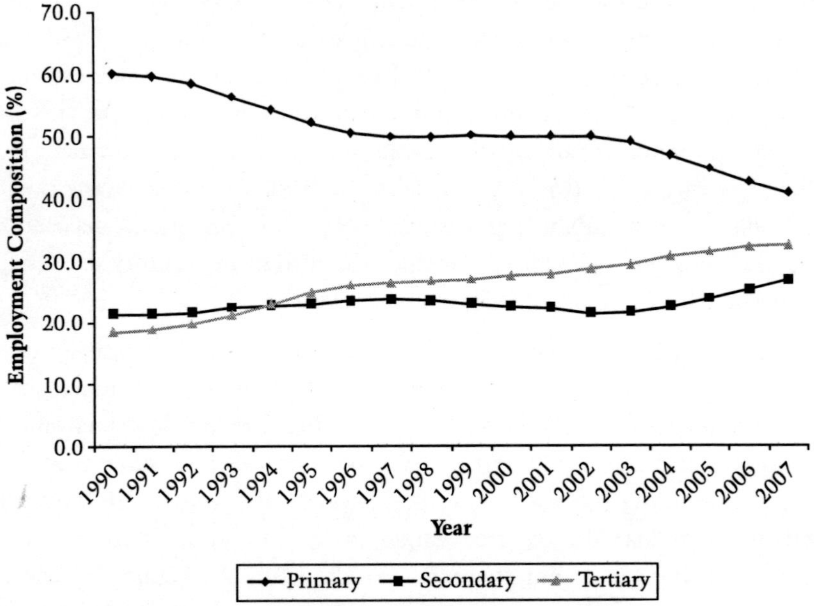

Source: NBS, China Statistical Yearbook (various years), China Statistical Press.

Figure 3.3

Employment and Real Wage for Migrant Workers

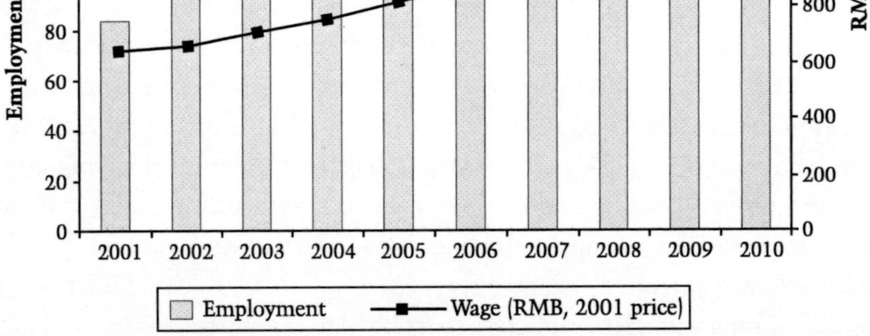

Source: Migrant Workers Monitoring Report in 2010, mimeo.

Migrant workers have been the main source of the increase in labour supply in the urban labour market during the past decades. In recent years, in addition to the growth in employment of migrants, their average monthly earnings have been increasing. For instance, the annual growth rate of real monthly earnings (at 2001 prices) for migrant workers was 19.6 per cent in 2008. In 2009, despite the global financial crisis, we still see an increase in both employment and wages for migrant workers. In 2010, as one of the outcomes of economic recovery, the average real monthly earnings for migrant workers increased by 15.5 per cent.

During the previous era with a dual economic structure, the labour force that was transferred from rural areas increased its productivity, whether working in manufacturing or services. Therefore, labour re-allocation from low to high productivity sectors resulted in an improvement in economic efficiency, which contributed to overall economic growth. Previous studies have demonstrated that labour mobility between rural and urban areas contributed 16-20 per cent to overall economic growth during the first two decades of the reform period (Cai and Wang, 1999). After China passed through the Lewis turning point, the contribution of labour migration to overall economic growth declined, even though it is still an important factor driving growth. From 2001 to 2009, its average contribution to overall economic growth was 16.7 per cent, and it has been decreasing in recent years (Cai, *et al.*, 2010). But overall, rural-to-urban migration has been a key characteristic of the labour market in recent decades, together with fast employment growth and economic transition. When aiming to improve the welfare of workers, policy-makers have to be concerned with the needs of migrant workers, as an indispensable component of the urban labour market.

The Social Protection System in China

Informality in the Chinese Labour Market

Although total employment has been increasing, the Chinese labour market also exhibits the informality that is generally considered to be one of the significant features of a developing labour market. The trend of informality in China has been changing since China started its market reform. It is believed that both urban economic restructuring and rural-to-urban migration have contributed to informality in the urban labour market. However, due to data limitations, it is difficult to measure the trend of informality using public data sources. As an alternative, Cai and Wang suggest that the difference between total employment and aggregate employment by sector in published NBS data could be considered as an approximate estimate of the amount of informal employment. If this 'employment residual' approach is applied, the urban informal sector accounted for 31.5 per cent of urban employment in 2008 while the corresponding figure was 36.1 per cent in 2005. Informality in the urban labour market mostly concerns migrant workers. According to a 2010 report by the National Bureau of Statistics, if the self-employed and wage employed without contract are defined as informal workers, 60 per cent of the migrant workers worked informally in 2009.

However, there is no nationally representative data at the micro level to measure the overall size of informal employment in the urban labour market and to distinguish its components. Here, the three waves of the China

Figure 3.4

The Size and Components of Informal Employment in the Urban Labour Market (%)

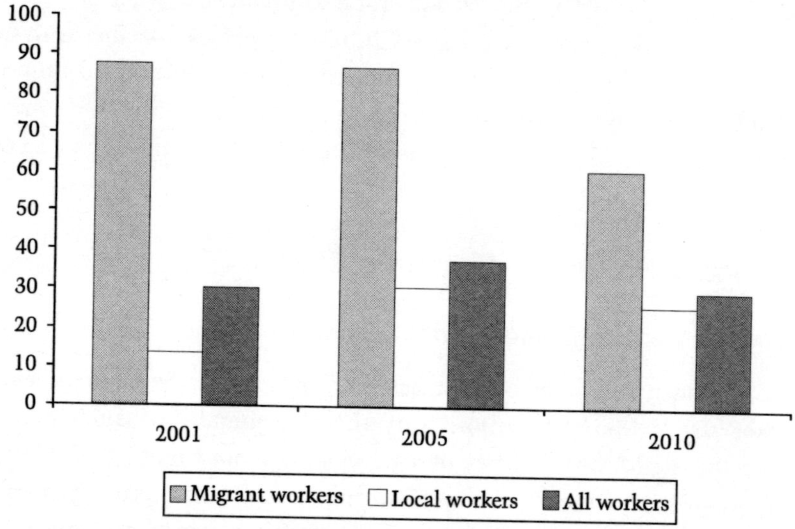

Source: Authors' calculation from CULS data.

Urban Labour Survey are used to look at the changing trend of informality in urban China. As Figure 3.4 shows, overall informal employment in the sampled cities increased from 2001 to 2005 and then decreased up to 2010.

Figure 3.4 also characterizes the labour market development at different stages. For instance, between 2001 and 2005, increased informality consisted mostly of increases in informal employment of urban local workers due to the restructuring of SOEs. From 2005 to 2010, the decline in informality was mostly accounted for by the increased formality of migrant workers, as a result of stricter labour market regulation. This trend also implies that employment quality might have improved during the past years, a question on which the next sections provide some empirical evidence.

The Framework of the Social Protection System

In order to deal with informality, the Chinese Government has made great efforts to construct a social protection system. Although informality concerns both rural migrant workers and local workers, the construction of the social protection system was firstly initiated to protect the workers with urban *hukou* (registration) suffering from labour market dislocations in 1990s. Since 1998, the Government has been trying to establish and improve the three social safety nets, comprising a guarantee of basic living expenses for workers laid off from SOEs, and unemployment insurance and *dibao*[3] for urban residents. Under the umbrella of the re-employment service centre of SOEs, laid-off workers can receive the basic living allowance, which is jointly paid by the Government, enterprises and the communities, and provided by the re-employment centre along with other employment services, including information and training. Those laid-off workers and other unemployed persons who fail to get re-employed after they leave the centre, can, according to regulations, receive unemployment insurance compensation for up to two years if they have participated in the unemployment insurance programme and paid the premium in full. Those laid-off and unemployed workers with a per capita family income lower than the local *dibao* line, as discussed later on in this paper, can enjoy the minimum living standard subsidy of urban residents, according to regulations.

When the negative shocks to the urban labour market disappeared during the early years of this century, a preliminary social protection framework in urban areas had thus been established. Thanks to the improving fiscal capacity at the national level and the fact that increasing resources have been available for expanding the social protection system, the Chinese Government has been able to raise new social programmes so as to cover more vulnerable people, in particular rural people. Figure 3.5 depicts the framework of the current social protection system in China. It includes both social insurance and social assistance programmes, which are characterized as contributory and non-contributory, respectively. For the social assistance programme, *dibao* has played a dominant role in terms of both the coverage and the benefit transferred. The social insurance system in urban areas is quite comprehensive; meanwhile, a series of new programmes has been implemented in rural areas, though participants only get limited benefits as compared to those in urban programmes.

Due to the gradualism that is applied to the construction of social protection, the current system is far from complete and is subject to adjustment, improvement, or further reforms. Several features of this system are worth noting here.

The most significant feature of the current social protection system in China is its segmentation between rural and urban areas. Given the legacy of the dual society, the gap of social protection between urban and rural areas was substantial. Although some new programmes, for instance, the New Cooperative Medical System, Rural Pension System, etc., have been implemented, the disparities in social protection between rural and urban areas are still obvious. Nevertheless, to some extent, the rural residents have been better off since the introduction of the new social protection programmes mentioned above. Meanwhile, China has been facing the challenge of integrating different systems and reducing the gaps in benefits among different groups of people. The segmentation may translate into differentiation of job quality, as we will see below.

The second feature is segmentation across various branches of the Government. As China started prioritizing social protection as one of the most important Government functions, different Government agencies began to raise new programmes in succession, which increases the coordination costs. For example, the rural medical system is run by the Ministry of Health, while the urban healthcare system is administered by

Figure 3.5

The Structure of the Social Protection System in China

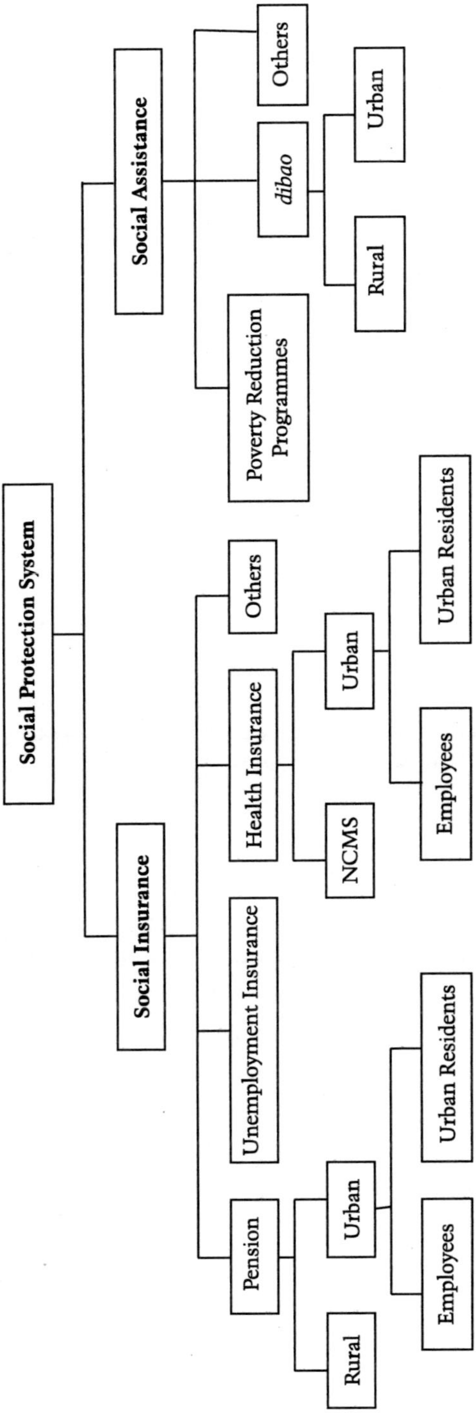

the Ministry of Human Resources and Social Security. Another example is that, in addition to the rural pension programmes, the Commission of Population and Family Planning initiated a special programme aiming to support the parents of one-child families.

In addition, the interaction between central and local governments in the construction of the social protection system is worth noting. Most social protection programmes are funded by both central and local governments. Given the disparities in economic development across regions, it is easy to understand that people in some poor areas are less protected due to limited fiscal capacity at local level. Furthermore, this leads to segmentation across regions because the rich areas tend to keep the benefit locally.

The Pillar of Social Assistance: The Dibao System

The Minimum Living Standard Guarantee Programme, the so-called *dibao* programme, is one of the most important pillars of social assistance in China. The programme directly targets the poor without considering their employment status. In 1993, Shanghai was the first city to introduce the *dibao* programme in order to support the poor, those whose income was below the official poverty line. The Central Government positively evaluated Shanghai's experiment. During the next year, the Ministry of Civil Affairs proposed to extend Shanghai's practice to the other urban areas of China. All cities and the towns where county governments were located were required to set up the programme as from 1999. In 2003, the Ministry of Civil Affairs claimed that in 2002, the *dibao* programme had covered all the urban poor whose income was below the local *dibao* line. As Figure 3.6 shows, the number of the poor covered by *dibao* increased dramatically after 1999, and has been stable since 2002. In 2008, 22.33 million urban residents were covered by *dibao* and the average per capita *dibao* transfer was 141 yuan. However, the *dibao* programme has been implemented on the basis of the locality of *hukou*, which means that migrants have been excluded from the programme despite their inclusion in urban population statistics.

Taking advantage of urban household survey data, it is possible to look at the income transfer of the *dibao* programme and its transitioning role in the social assistance system. Figure 3.7 plots the distribution of transfers

Figure 3.6

The Coverage and Level of Dibao: 1999-2008

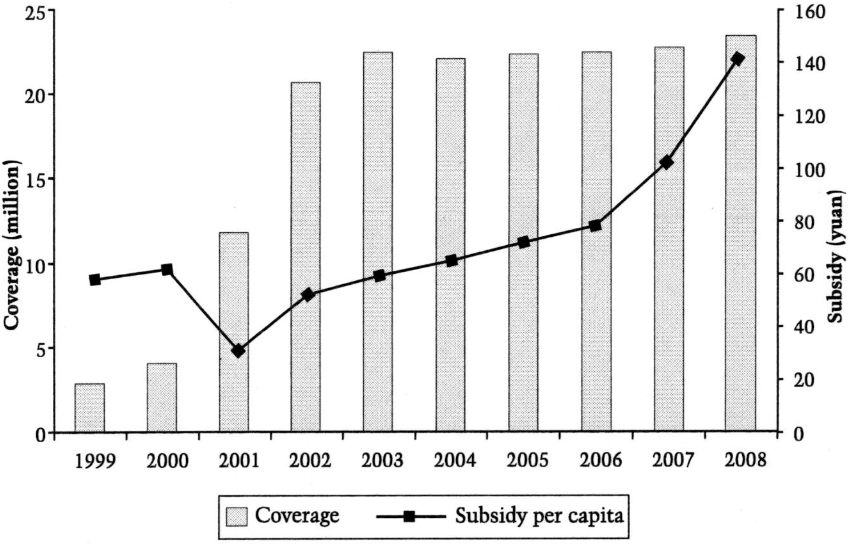

Source: Ministry of Civil Affairs, Statistics Report of Civil Affairs, various years.

based on the two rounds of household survey data for 2001 and 2005. The horizontal axis in the figure is the cumulative distribution of households by income per capita before transfer. The curves show the distribution of the cumulative amount of transfer to households and each curve represents one of the programmes, which are *dibao*, *xiagang* (the laid-off subsidy), and unemployment insurance, respectively. The two survey rounds show different patterns. In 2001, the three curves have a similar shape. For example, the poorest 20 per cent of the individuals got about 35 per cent of the unemployment transfers, about 40 per cent of the *xiagang* subsidy, and 55 per cent of the *dibao* transfers. This means that in 2001 the system of social assistance was not systematic, and the roles of different programmes were not clear. In addition, they had mixed functions. In 2005, however, the *dibao* curve was more concave than in 2001, but this is not the case for other two. The poorest 20 per cent of the individuals got about 25 per cent of the unemployment transfers, about 25 per cent of the *xiagang* subsidy, and more than 80 per cent of the *dibao* transfers. This also indicates that *dibao* has become the dominant social assistance programme in urban China.

Figure 3.7

Concentration Curves of Income Transfer Programmes

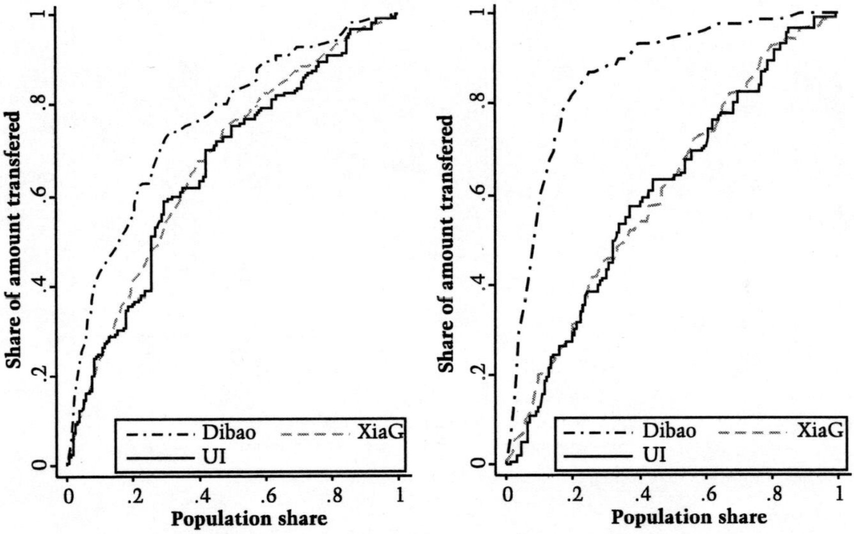

Note: The year for the left-hand graph is 2001, and for the right-hand graph is 2005.

Source: China Urban Labour Market Survey, Institute of Population and Labor Economics, CASS.

As noted earlier, the *dibao* programme is also segmented between rural and urban areas. Since the end of the 1990s, China has implemented the *dibao* programme in rural areas. By 2007, the programme had been implemented all over rural China. The coverage of the programme in rural areas has been increasing (Figure 3.8). The number of beneficiaries increased from 2.66 million in 1999 to 35.66 million in 2007, and the number of households under the programme increased from 1.57 million in 2002 to 16.09 million in 2007. The average monthly subsidy was 70 yuan in 2007. Nevertheless, it is clear that efforts need to be made to bridge the gap between rural and urban areas, even within the programme.

Figure 3.8

Increasing Coverage of the Rural Dibao System

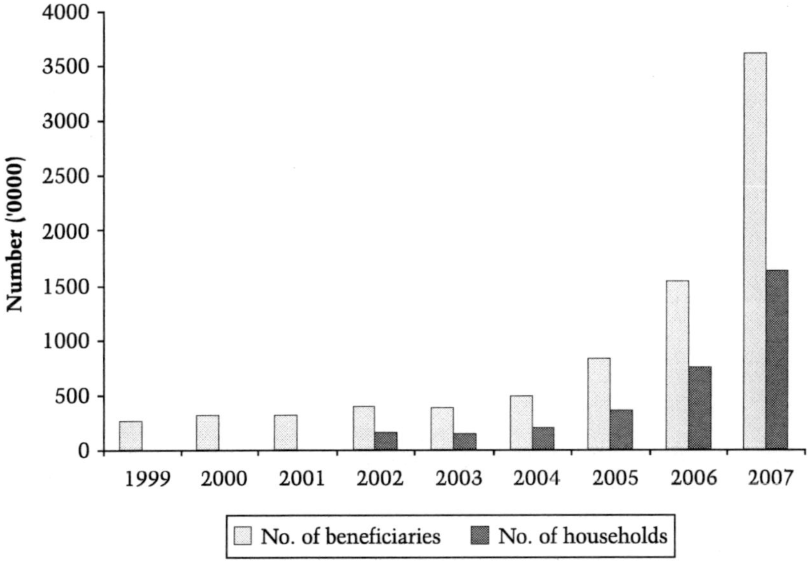

Source: Ministry of Civil Affairs, China Civil Affairs Statistical Yearbook (various years), China Statistical Press, Beijing.

Protecting the Elderly

Due to its rapid demographic transition, China has already become an aging society even though economic development is still at a low level. Among the social protection programmes, therefore, the system to support the elderly is the most important and pressing one to be constructed. In order to deal with the challenge of an aging society, China has to widen the scope of the pension system to support more old people. The current urban pension system is Pay-As-You-Go, because the workers who had long careers in SOEs actually have no accumulation for their pensions. For this reason, increasing the coverage of the pension system has been one of the key elements for the establishment of the social security system. As Figure 3.9 shows, in the new century the total number of participants in the pension system has been increasing, reaching 187.7 million in 2006. Meanwhile, the total number of retirees with pension, the number of men over 60 and women over 55 years of age, has also increased steadily with the aging of the population.

Figure 3.9

Increasing Coverage of the Urban Pension System

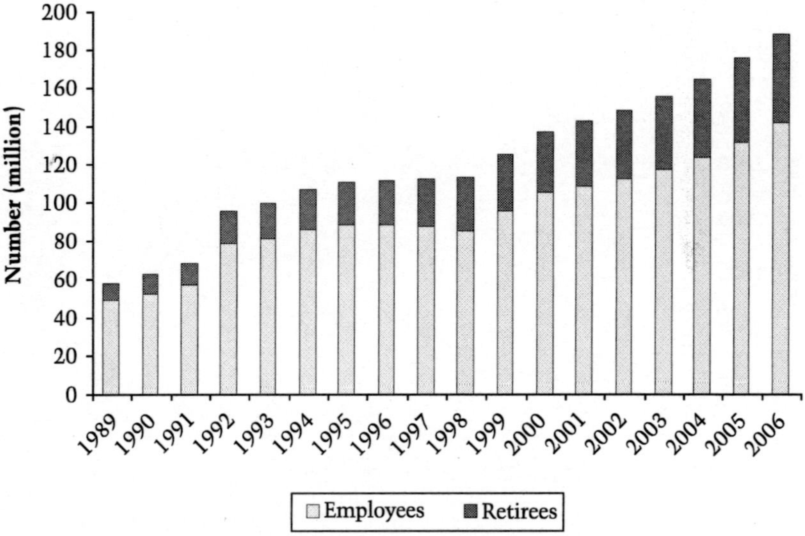

Source: NBS, China Statistical Yearbook (2007), China Statistical Press, Beijing.

Since the early 1990s, a rural pension system has been introduced on an experimental basis in some counties. By the end of 1992, more than 700 counties had established a framework of regulation for a rural social pension system, nearly 20 counties had established basic rural old-age pension systems which covered all the farmers, and more than 35 million rural people participated in this programme. By 1994, 28 provinces, autonomous regions and municipalities had counties piloting the rural old-age pension system.

The administration of the rural pension system was transferred from the Ministry of Civil Affairs to the Ministry of Labour and Social Security in 1998, when the government organization reform was carried out. In July 1999, the State Council pointed out that rural areas have no capability to construct a universal pension system and decided to stop accepting more people for participation in the system. Areas with enough capability would transfer gradually to a commercial pension insurance.

In 2002, the report to the 16th National Congress of the Communist Party of China provided guidance for the construction of the rural pension system. Two documents, *Regulations by The Central Committee and the State Council on Encouraging Socialist New Countryside*, and the *Eleventh-Five-Year Plan*, proposed that China should establish a rural old-age pension system which is compatible with the economic development level of rural areas.

In recent years, the rural pension system has been piloted by various regions. Unlike the urban pension system, which has a mature and nationally universal plan, the rural pension system has been at the experimental stage with large variations in terms of programme design, level of benefit, level of pooling, and coverage rates.

In 2009, the Central Government formally promoted a pension programme for rural areas after pilots at local level for years. The State Council issued *Suggestions on Launching New Rural Pension Programmes* in September 2009. According to the *Suggestions*, 10 per cent of the counties were to pilot the programme in 2009 and the programme would cover all rural areas in 2020. Combined with household support, land tenure,[4] and social relief, the objective is to support the rural elderly. In practice, the programmes have been introduced more rapidly than planned.

Migrant workers constitute a special group of people working in the urban areas with rural identity. Although they are eligible for the rural pension programme, the coverage rate of the pension programme for migrant workers in urban areas is very low, while the rural programmes are not able to meet their demand. There exists controversy about the directions of pension programmes for migrant workers. It seems undesirable to simply apply the current urban plan to migrant workers due to their mobility. However, exclusion of migrants from the urban pension system would maintain the social gap between those migrants and urban residents.

Integrating Social Protection Programmes

Thanks to gradual reforms, China is on the way to implementing a complete social safety net at the price of segmented social programmes. It is widely accepted that the integration of social programmes is the key issue for improving China's social safety nets in the near future, which includes reforms in several areas discussed below.

The inequality of access to social security results in welfare gaps between residents with rural and urban identities, which is also a drawback of the current system that is widely criticized. Due to the limitation of fiscal affordability, it has not been possible to provide universal social security and social services for rural residents. Even though some social programmes have started in rural areas, they still provide much lower benefits than urban programmes. However, with increasing fiscal revenue, it is time to discuss how to integrate rural people into a modern social security system.

Lack of portability has been one of the most essential shortcomings of current social programmes for a long time, and this also becomes a barrier that limits labour mobility across regions. Social programmes piloted by local governments have a very low level of pooling, which makes it difficult to transfer individual accounts between regions. In recent years, it has been quite frequent for migrant workers to withdraw their contributions from the social security system when they decide to move to other places.

The gradual reforms have also brought up the issue of coordination between social programmes. In China, specific social programmes are managed by different government agencies, which has increased the difficulties of coordination between programmes. For example, different means are used to provide social assistance to the poor in rural and urban areas. Rural poverty is basically targeted at the regional level, and poverty reduction is achieved through regional economic development. Unlike rural poverty, the social assistance for the urban poor is targeted at households through the *dibao* programme. Owing to the difference of policies between rural and urban areas, especially the discrepancy in the level of subsidy between the two regions, it is hard for local city governments to include migrants in their social safety nets. These factors lead to segmented poverty alleviation policies between urban and rural China.

Inequality and Its Trend

It is widely observed that since the economic reform and opening-up policy initiated in the late 1970s, while China has achieved unprecedentedly fast economic growth, its income distribution has widened (World Bank, 2009; CDRF, 2005; Ravallion and Chen, 2007).

No matter what measurements are employed by researchers, they all indicate that inequalities in both income and consumption among rural and urban residents have increased during most of the reform period, and the myth of relatively lower income inequality in China by international standards has been proven to be mistaken (Gibson, *et al.*, 2001). The nationwide Gini coefficient of per capita income increased from 0.31 in 1981 to 0.447 in 2001 (Ravallion and Chen, 2007) and/or 0.46 in 2002 (Khan and Riskin, 2005). This degree of income inequality is indeed relatively high, as compared with both China's own past and with the general tendency in other countries (CDRF, 2005).

A more detailed examination (Ravallion and Chen, 2007) reveals that the Gini coefficient of per capita income among rural residents increased from 0.25 in 1981 to 0.37 in 2001, while the Gini coefficient of per capita income among urban residents increased from 0.19 in 1981 to 0.33 in 2001. During each of the periods, the overall Gini coefficient of income[5]— that is, 0.31 in 1981, 0.35 in 1990 and 0.45 in 2001—was higher than that in either rural or urban areas, implying the existence of a large and increasing income gap between rural and urban areas.

Using the same data set and methodology as used by Ravallion and Chen (2007), the recent report by the World Bank (2009) extends the estimation of the national Gini coefficient to 2005. The result indicates that the Gini coefficient of income inequality rose to 0.453 in 2003 and slightly dropped to 0.443 in 2005, when controlling for the difference in the cost of living. The World Bank report (2009) also indicates that the spatial variation in the cost of living makes a difference in measuring income inequality. Adjusted for the spatial cost of living, the Gini index dropped from 0.453 to 0.411 in 2005.

Although it is widely reported that overall income inequality and the difference between rural and urban incomes in China have reached historically high levels, it is hard to believe that China can maintain a stable society to support fast economic growth when the media report such high inequality levels. Since many studies have found that increasing inequality may be detrimental to economic growth (Persson and Tabellini, 1994; Alesina and Rodrik, 1994; Clarke, 1995; Sabot, *et al.*, 1998; Rodrik, 1999), it is hard to explain the co-existence of big income gaps and the fastest economic growth in the world. In particular, Rodrik (1999) points out that the countries with the most unequal income distribution had been suffering the lowest economic growth since 1975. In this regard, it is likely that either the inequality prior to the reform was underestimated or the inequality trend in China was overestimated for some reason.

In order to understand income inequality in China correctly, some unique aspects of the Chinese market and statistical system need to be addressed. As a transition economy with fast economic growth, the stories of both reform and development complicate the issue of inequality. Therefore, before going through the inequality issues, it is important to understand the institutional changes that have taken place over the reform period.

Since the 1980s, the household responsibility system has been introduced into rural China, which significantly improved the incentives for rural households in agricultural input. With the consequent manifold increase of the work effort, there was a significant decline in the labour time needed for agriculture, and a labour surplus emerged. In order to absorb this surplus, peasant households, which now had operational autonomy, firstly switched their work from being used solely for grain production to other agricultural sectors, and then from cultivation to the overall development of agriculture, forestry, animal husbandry, fisheries and household sideline production, greatly changing the agricultural production structure, and improving labour utilization and income levels. With the improvement in agricultural productivity, however, the capacity of both cultivation and 'big agriculture' (including farming, forestry, animal husbandry, sideline production and fisheries) to absorb labour was ultimately limited.

The gradual abolition of institutional obstacles has been the key to increased labour mobility. Observing the narrowing capacity to absorb surplus labour in the rural sectors, in 1983 the Government began to allow farmers to engage in long distance transport and marketing of their products beyond local marketplaces. This was the first time that Chinese farmers had obtained legitimate rights to do business outside their home towns. In 1984, the regulations were further relaxed, and farmers were encouraged by the State to work in nearby small towns. A major policy reform took place in 1988, when the Central Government allowed farmers to work in enterprises or to run their own business in cities under the condition that they were self-sufficient in food.[6]

In the 1990s, the Central Government and local governments all applied a series of measures, which relaxed policies restricting migration, implying a certain degree of reform in the household registration system at each stage of the reform process. During this period, policies towards labour mobility across regions diverged. The divergence can be found first between central and local governments. As regards employment, income and social security in the country as a whole, the Central Government encouraged labour migration between rural and urban areas, and across provincial borders, while attitudes towards migration of local governments differed between the sending and receiving places. In relatively poor regions with a high proportion of surplus labourers and a high share of agriculture, policies towards labour migration have been encouraging and supportive, and the governments have taken measures to help farmers move out to seek better jobs and higher wages. The more advanced regions, however, are more concerned with the security of local employment, and welcome migrant workers only when local economies need extra workers. In those regions, policies towards inflows of migrants change cyclically as employment pressures facing local governments change over time, that is, each time the local unemployment problems become severe, they tend to take measures to displace migrant workers (Cai, *et al.*, 2001). With labour market developments, the situations have changed over time.

By the twenty-first century, the decision-making power for timely reform of the household registration system was actually devolved to local, in particular urban governments. At the time, the policy orientations of migrant-receiving regions diverged as well. While it must be recognized that the legitimacy of migration policies is based on the *hukou* system, in reality, the institutional factors restricting the flow of labour are not confined to the *hukou* system itself. Considering the costs and benefits of policies related to social security provisioning, social welfare and other public services underlying the *hukou* system, two types of local government have changed their rejectionist attitude towards migration, because they do not expect adverse effects on local welfare. The first kind is those fast-growing cities that have significantly benefited from the ample supply of migrant workers. The second is those whose local budgetary ability is severely constrained so that the provisions of public services have been too limited for them to worry about the inclusion of migrants.

Many researchers have tried to relate widening income inequality with institutional restrictions on labour mobility. For example, by combining the Lewis model with a price scissors model, Knight and Song (1999) described a distorted rural–urban relationship, characterized by a large income gap and conditioned by the unlimited supply of labour. Yang and Cai (2003) examined the changes in institutions influencing labour mobility and their impact on the rural–urban income gap. Labour migration means that people move from low productivity agriculture to non-agricultural sectors with higher productivity. Through the convergence of the marginal productivity of labour between the agricultural and non-agricultural sectors, the rural–urban income gap is expected to be narrowed. Logically, Chinese economists tend to believe that with the elimination of institutional barriers deterring migration, the persistent income gap can eventually be reduced by full labour mobility across regions and sectors.

For example, based on a simulation, Whalley and Zhang (2004) suggest that once the obstacles imposed by the *hukou* system to prevent free migration of labour are abolished, all the existing income inequality between rural and urban areas would disappear. Here, their relatively strong assumption is that the *hukou* system is the single important obstacle to labour migration. Lin *et al.* (2004) estimate a response elasticity of migration to the income gap and conclude that migration is indeed a mechanism for narrowing the income gap. In the meantime, they also suggest that the present scale of migration is not adequate to reduce the existing income gap because of the presence of the *hukou* system and fast growth in coastal areas.

In addition to the factors mentioned above, regional disparities have contributed to overall inequality over the past decades. Considering that individual income is determined, to some extent, by the level of local economic development, regional disparities would translate into household income inequality. Estimates based on large nationally representative samples indicate that the provincial disparities contributed 23.4 per cent to overall income inequality in 1995 and 12.9 per cent in 2003 (World Bank, 2009).

Although regional economic disparities cannot explain the whole story of household income inequality, it is good to know the trend in regional disparities, which constitute one of the important determinants of household income gaps. In the 1980s, the economic reform was focused on reforming the microeconomic system in both rural and urban areas, which improved the technical efficiency of micro-units and thus had wider effects on economic growth. The coastal areas, where the growth potential had been suppressed before the reform, caught up quickly in the 1980s. Based on provincial data released by the National Bureau of Statistics, it can be observed that the Gini coefficient of per capita GDP among provinces dropped from 0.347 in 1978 to 0.268 in 1990. The two coefficients are 0.241 and 0.213,[7] respectively, if weighted by population (Figure 3.10).

Figure 3.10

Gini and Theil Index of Provincial per Capita GDP: 1978-2008

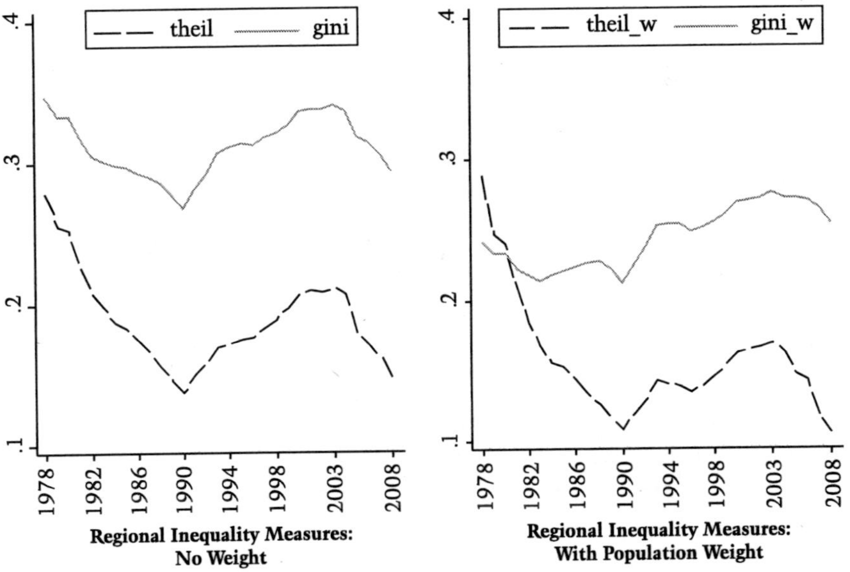

Source: National Bureau of Statistics (NBS), China Statistical Yearbook (various years), China Statistical Press, Beijing.

In 1992, the Chinese Government formally accepted the concept of market economy and initiated the reforms of the macroeconomic system. Since then, provincial economic performance has been determined by allocative efficiency. As a result, the regional disparities have increased because the coastal areas maintained high rates of growth and the rest of

China lagged behind. In 2003, the Gini coefficient of per capita GDP among provinces peaked at 0.34 (0.277 if weighted by population).

In many economies, for instance, the United States, Japan and other OECD countries, the contribution of regional inequality to overall inequality is observed to decrease with economic development (Barro and Sala-i-Martin, 1995). It seems that the Chinese economy has displayed a similar pattern since the regional disparities started declining after 2003. Thanks to a series of regional development strategies implemented in the new century, for example, Western Development Strategies, Plan of Revitalizing Northeast China, and Plan of Rising Central China, the Gini coefficient of per capita GDP among provinces dropped to 0.29 in 2008. If we take the early 1990s, when China formally accepted the market economy system, as the starting point, Figure 3.10 presents an inverted U shape pattern since 1990 that is a typical Kuznets curve.

Increased inequality partly reflects the economic reform that corrects the distorted economic system. For instance, a number of studies (for example, Zhang, *et al.*, 2005) find that the returns to education in the Chinese labour market have been increasing during the reform period, which implies that the egalitarianism embedded in the economic planning system has been reformed. In turn, this effect would translate into increased inequality. Goh, *et al.* (2008) find that the earnings difference between skilled and unskilled workers explains most of the increase in inequality during the period from 1989 to 2004. Sicular, *et al.* (2007) show that 25-30 per cent of the income inequality between urban and rural China could be attributed to the difference in education. In this regard, part of the increased inequality is understandable and the policy to contain inequality should be focused on providing more equal opportunities for human capital accumulation rather than on the outcomes *per se*.

Given the importance of labour income in income formation, the labour market institutions and then the labour market outcomes have direct links with income inequality. A more equal earnings distribution in the labour market would tend to equalize the household income distribution. Since the 1990s, the Chinese labour market has witnessed substantial development, as evidenced by increasing total employment, significant sectoral shifts, and institutional changes. Each of these components of labour market development has an impact on trends in inequality. Both the urban household survey and the rural household survey show the importance for households of incomes from the labour market. Figure 3.11 shows the share of wage income from the labour market as a proportion of household income in both rural and urban areas. Before the radical reform of the urban labour market in the mid-1990s, full employment in urban areas had been guaranteed. That is why we see more than three-quarters of incomes for urban households coming from the labour market. Urban economic restructuring and the development of the capital market have diversified the sources of urban household income.[8] Even so, labour income still accounted for two-thirds of urban household income in 2008. And thanks to rural-to-urban migration, wage income has become more and more important for rural households. The proportion of wage income in the net income of rural households almost doubled from 1990 to 2008.

Figure 3.11

The Share of Labour Income in Household Incomes

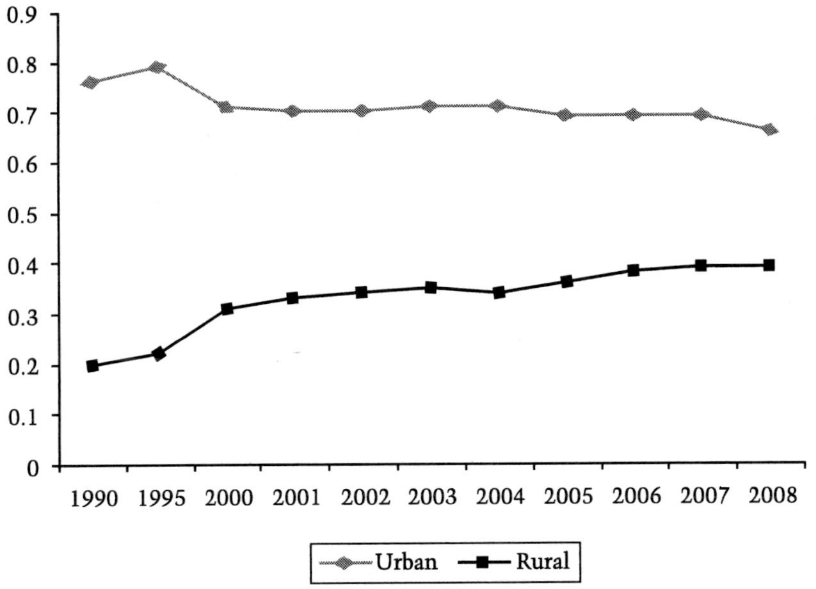

Source: National Bureau of Statistics (NBS), China Statistical Yearbook (various years), China Statistical Press, Beijing.

Although it is too early to observe a substantial turning point in the trend towards increasing income inequality, there are some indications that the income gaps are starting to be bridged.

First of all, wages for unskilled workers have been increasing substantially in recent years. This trend has been reinforced in recent years since the Chinese labour market passed the Lewis turning point and migrant workers began to see their wage rates grow after two decades of stagnation. Figure 3.12 presents the annual growth rate of wages since 2002 and its acceleration in recent years, both in real and nominal terms. Meanwhile, labour shortage appeared frequently. Even with the shock from the global financial crisis, the average monthly wage for migrants reached a historically high 1334 yuan in 2008, 55 per cent of average earnings in urban units, and 19.6 per cent more than the previous year in real terms. It is reasonable to believe that the wage growth for the low-income group of migrants helps reduce the gap between urban and rural residents. In 2010, rural households had a faster growth in incomes than urban households.

Figure 3.12

Annual Wage Growth Rates for Migrant Workers

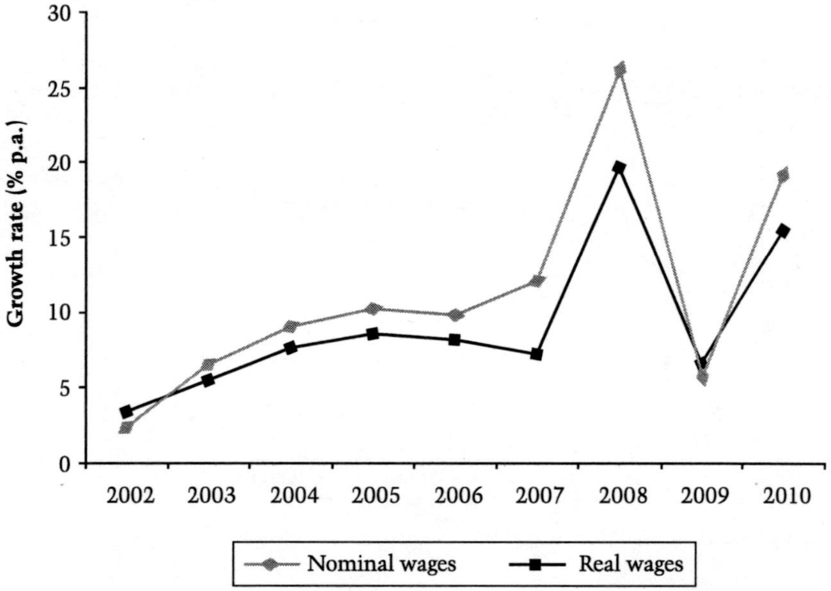

Source: Authors' calculation based on data from Statistical Reports of National Bureau of Statistics (NBS).

Second, previous estimations of overall income inequality are subject to sampling bias. As pointed out by Park (2008), current measurements of inequality are subject to a number of sources of bias, including sampling bias, exclusion of some categories of income, classification of rural and urban areas, and differences in the cost of living. Some previous studies have already noted that rural–urban migration created sources of bias when measuring income inequality. Until 2002, the NBS urban sample excluded migrants living in urban areas. After they were included, they represented less than 2 per cent of the sample (Park, 2008), even though the 2005 1 per cent Population Sampling Survey found that 22 per cent of the population living in cities were migrants. Using rural data from 19 provinces and urban data from 11 provinces, Sicular and others (2007) find that including migrants in calculating urban per capita income reduces the urban–rural income ratio from 2.27:1 to 2.12:1. Ravallion and Chen (2007) also realized that rural–urban migration could be a source of bias in the calculation of inequality though their measurement was based on the urban and rural household surveys.

Third, it seems that recent institutional changes in the labour market have helped equalize income distribution. With the sustained and rapid economic development and aging of the population, the era of unlimited labour supply has come to an end and structural labour shortages have emerged. This has created good opportunities to protect the legal rights and interests of labourers. Under these circumstances, China has accelerated the construction of labour market institutions. A series of labour market institutions and policies have been put into place recently, including the *Employment Contract Law*, the *Labour Disputes Mediation and Arbitration Law*, the *Wage Guideline System*, the *Minimum Wage Regulations* and the *Employment Promotion Law*. In addition, the Chinese Government has proposed both active and passive labour market programmes to respond to labour market fluctuations. During a period with robust employment demand, these new regulations may not have a negative effect in reducing total employment but may increase workers' earnings significantly. Empirical research (Cai *et al.*, 2010) also indicates that recent institutional changes in the labour market actually promote the equalization of incomes.

Conclusions

As the largest developing country, China has to provide enough job opportunities to make use of its most plentiful resources. During the past three decades, the development path in China has followed the typical economic development strategy by exploiting its advantage in labour. Through the expansion of labour-intensive sectors, China has succeeded in transferring the surplus labour out of agriculture, which contributes to overall economic growth. When the movement of the labour force out of rural areas and the outcomes of demographic transition are translated into the labour market, it can be seen that China has passed the Lewis turning point, as evidenced by frequent labour shortages and rising wages for unskilled workers.

With the country passing through this turning point, it is time to put into place institutional arrangements to promote social protection. Firstly, the substantial transition in the labour market makes it possible for workers to bargain for their rights. Secondly, employers tend to compete for labour and are willing to provide more protection due to the scarcity of labour. Thirdly, as the country as a whole escapes from the poverty trap, the Government has the financial capacity to implement new social protection programmes.

Although it is widely accepted that China is facing serious income inequality, the on-going labour market transition may play an active role in remedying the trend. The increasing wages for unskilled workers improve the income distribution at the bottom end of the labour market. Labour mobility between rural and urban areas bridges the gap between the two areas, considered as the most important source of overall inequality in China. In addition, the sampling bias in the data that were used in previous estimates of income inequality has to be taken into account, since it would tend to lead to an overestimation of inequality.

Even though the labour market situation has improved, institutional arrangements have to be put into place to deal with the implications of both the Lewis turning point and the Kuznets turning point. The experiences in China have already revealed the importance of social protection in constructing a harmonious society. Among the stakeholders building the social protection system, in particular, greater efforts from the Government may well be needed. When enterprises are challenged by the growing labour costs, the Government should shoulder more responsibility to finance new programmes.

China still has a long way to go to build an integrated social protection system. Increasing the coverage of social protection, especially for migrants, is of great importance for achieving inclusive growth under current situations. Right now, providing more protection for migrant workers is an important and pressing task. Due to the instability of migrants' employment and high contribution rates of various social security programmes, there is lack of incentives for both migrant workers and their employers to participate in those programmes, resulting in their low coverage. These exclusions from labour market institutions and social protection expose migrants to labour market risks and prevent them from fulfilling the role of a stable, central force of the urban labour market. Migrant workers' needs should thus be at the centre of labour market institutions and the social security system.

References

Alesina, Alberto and Dani Rodrik (1994). "Distributive Politics and Economic Growth", *Quarterly Journal of Economics* 109(2): 465-90. May.

Barro, Robert J. and Xavier Sala-i-Martin (1995). *Economic Growth*. New York: McGraw-Hill.

Cai, Fang (ed.) (2009). *The Developments in Labor and Social Security of China in the Past Three Decades*. Beijing: Economic Management Press.

Cai, Fang and Wang Dewen (1999). "The Sustainability of Economic Growth and the Labour Contribution", *Economic Research Journal* (Jingji yanjiu) 10: 62-68.

Cai, Fang, Yang Du and Meiyan Wang (2001). "*Hukou* System and Labor Market Discrimination", *Journal of Economic Research* 11.

Cai, Fang, Yang Du and Meiyan Wang (2010). "Migration and Poverty Reduction", (*mimeo*).

China Development Research Foundation (CDRF) (2005). *China Human Development Report 2005: Towards Human Development with Equity.* Beijing: China Translation and Publishing Corporation.

Clarke, R. (1995). "More Evidence on Income Distribution and Growth", *Journal of Development Economics* 47: 403-27.

Du, Yang and Meiyan Wang (2011). "Employment and Its Structure in China: Re-estimation and Implications", in Fang Cai (ed.), *Report on Population and Labor Issues in China*. Beijing: Social Science Academic Press.

Gibson, J., J. Huang and S. Rozelle (2001). "Why Is Income Inequality So Low in China Compared to Other Countries? The Effect of Household Survey Method", *Economics Letters* 71: 329-33.

Goh, C., X. Luo and N. Zhu (2008). "Income Growth, Inequality and Poverty Reduction: A Case Study of Eight Provinces in China", *China Economic Review* 20(3): 485-96.

Khan, A.R. and C. Riskin (2005). "China's Household Income and Its Distribution, 1995 and 2002", *China Quarterly* 182: 356–84.

Knight, John and Lina Song (1999). *The Rural–Urban Divide, Economic Disparities and Interactions in China*. Oxford and New York: Oxford University Press.

Lin, Justin, Gewei Wang and Yaohui Zhao (2004). "Regional Inequality and Labor Transfers in China", *Economic Development and Cultural Change* 52: 587-603. April.

Park, A. (2008). "Rural–Urban Inequality in China", in S. Yusuf and T. Saich (eds), *China Urbanizes*. Washington, D.C.: World Bank.

Persson, T. and G. Tabellini (1994). "Is Inequality Harmful for Growth? Theory and Evidence", in *American Economic Review* 84(3): 600-21.

Ravallion, Martin and Shaohua Chen (2007). "China's (Uneven) Progress against Poverty", *Journal of Development Economics* 82: 1-42.

Rodrik, D. (1999). "Where Did All the Growth Go? External Shocks, Social Conflict and Growth Collapses", *Journal of Economic Growth* 4: 385- 412.

Sabot, R., T.C. Pinckney and N. Birdsall (1998). "Why Low Inequality Spurs Growth: Savings and Investment by the Poor", in A. Solimano (ed.), *Social Inequalities: Values, Growth and the State*. Ann Arbor: University of Michigan Press.

Sicular, Terry, Ximing Yue, Björn Gustafsson, and Shi Li (2007), "The Urban–Rural Income Gap and Inequality in China", *Review of Income and Wealth* 53(1): 93-126.

Whalley, John and Shuming Zhang (2004), "Inequality Change in China and (Hukou) Labour Mobility Restrictions", *NBER Working Paper* 10,683. Washington, D.C.: National Bureau of Economic Research.

World Bank (2009), *From Poor Areas to Poor People: China's Evolving Poverty Reduction Agenda, An Assessment of Poverty and Inequality in China*. Washington, D.C.: World Bank.

Yang, Dennis and Fang Cai (2003). "The Political Economy of China's Rural–Urban Divide" in Nicholas C. Hope, Dennis Tao Yang and Mu Yang Li (eds), *How Far across the River: Chinese Policy Reform at the Millennium*. Stanford, California: Stanford University Press.

Zhang, Junsen, Yaohui Zhao, Albert Park and Xiaoqing Song (2005), "Economic Returns to Schooling in Urban China, 1988-2001", *Journal of Comparative Economics* 33: 730-52.

Notes

1. Migrants are defined as those who lived outside the township for more than six months in the year.
2. According to the definition employed in the Chinese statistics system, only agriculture is counted as the primary sector.
3. *Dibao* is the Minimum Living Standard Guarantee programme; see more details on page 78.
4. Owning land is seen as one of the sources of support for the elderly.
5. As described by Ravallion and Chen (2007), the complete micro data are not available for any year. See the World Bank (2009) for the same discussion.

6. At the time, the rationing system had not been abolished and people without local *hukou* were not entitled to coupons for buying food and other necessities in the local market.
7. The developed coastal areas are also the most populous areas in China. Therefore, the inequality measures weighted by population are relatively smaller. This effect has been ignored by many studies.
8. According to the NBS definition, household incomes are divided into the following categories: wage incomes, asset incomes, transfer income, and business incomes.

4 Economic Growth, Employment and Social Protection in India

Ajit K. Ghose

Introduction

Development economists and policy planners (a very large majority of them at any rate) believed, until quite recently, that economic growth, confined largely to the organized (or formal or modern) sector of developing countries, would result in the progressive transfer of workers from the unorganized (or informal or traditional) to the organized sector.[1] Efforts were, therefore, made to create good conditions of employment in the organized sector while the unorganized sector was left to its own devices. If economic growth meant a steadily rising share of the organized sector in total employment in the economy, it was thought that a steadily growing section of the workforce would enjoy the good conditions of employment being created in the organized sector.

Social protection, in this vision, was among the elements of good conditions of employment in the organized sector; jobs in the organized sector came with an entitlement to social protection. As growth occurred, it was expected that the coverage of social protection would expand with the expansion of employment in the organized sector. The growth of the organized sector was also expected to generate some benefits for workers in the unorganized sector through spillover effects. The transfer of workers from the unorganized to the organized sector together with increased demand for the products of the unorganized sector would, it was believed, stimulate the growth of labour productivity in the unorganized sector. This would increase incomes and reduce poverty in the unorganized sector, thereby reducing the proportion of the population in desperate need of social assistance. Hence, it was believed that there was no pressing need to regard social protection as an independent objective of development policy. Indeed, pursuit of social protection as an independent objective, it was feared, would retard growth by lowering investment and hence would actually halt progress on all fronts, including extension of social protection coverage.

Unfortunately, the assumption that economic growth would result in the progressive transfer of workers from the unorganized to the organized sector turned out to be highly optimistic.[2] Many developing countries, including India, have achieved high rates of economic growth, but this growth has not been associated with a sustained process of labour transfer from the unorganized to the organized sector. Far from steadily rising, the share of the organized sector in total employment in the economy actually declined in India, as in many other developing countries. Moreover, informal employment was growing even in the organized sector in many cases so that the share of workers with access to social protection was declining within the organized sector itself. Good employment, and the coverage of social protection with it, simply failed to expand in the expected manner. Fortunately, the other assumption—that about spillover effects of growth in the organized sector—has proved to have been somewhat more realistic; poverty has declined in many developing countries mainly because labour productivity in the unorganized sector increased.[3]

Nevertheless, even after half a century of 'development', there remain huge unmet needs for both productive employment and social protection in most developing countries.[4] Moreover, the failure of the model has also underlined the need to regard both employment and social protection as independent objectives of development policy and thus to re-think growth strategies and to de-link social protection from employment. It is fairly clear that if the growth process fails altogether to generate a process of transfer of workers from the unorganized to the organized sector, it would prove difficult for governments to arrange decent levels of social protection for all workers even in the long run. On the other hand, it is also clear that even if the growth process can be suitably modified to generate a process of labour transfer (that is, a process whereby employment growth in the organized sector is faster than the labour force growth in the economy), a large majority of the workers would continue to be engaged in 'bad' jobs (and consequently in poverty) in the unorganized sector for a long time to come.

Social protection for these workers cannot be linked to their jobs, nor can these workers be left without any kind of social protection.[5]

This paper focuses mainly on the failure of the old vision through a scrutiny of the evolution of employment conditions in India during the period 1983-2005. Following on this, it casts a glance at some relatively recent initiatives by the Government that seek to provide a minimum level of social protection to workers in poor jobs.

Economic Growth and Employment in India, 1983-2005

The period 1983-2005 was a period of rapid economic growth in India. The period was also one of economic reforms. In the 1980s, the reforms were directed mainly towards the liberalization of the economy while in the 1990s, they were directed mainly towards opening up of the economy.[6] The rapid economic growth of the period is often attributed to these reforms that liberalized and opened up India's economy. This view, of course, has not gone unchallenged and a consensus has remained elusive. But these disputes and debates need not detain us here.

What is beyond dispute is that the rapid economic growth of the period did not generate a process of transformative change in employment conditions in the economy. In fact, the employment intensity of growth in the organized sector was already very low in the 1980s, and the opening up of the economy, contrary to expectation, lowered it further in the 1990s. In other words, economic growth failed to improve employment conditions through the usually envisioned mechanism—a process of transfer of labour from the unorganized to the organized sector. The share of the organized sector in total employment, in fact, declined quite significantly. As it happens, however, there was fairly rapid growth of the unorganized sector itself. This meant substantive growth of output per worker and hence some improvement of employment conditions in the sector, which was reflected in the decline in the incidence of extreme poverty. However, the same processes also resulted in the strengthening of dualism and growth of inequality. This briefly is the story that emerges from the analysis in this section.

The basic data relating to employment trends in India during the period 1983-2004/05 are presented in Table 4.1.[7] Before we discuss what these data show, however, we need to say something about the nature of the data and the definitions of the categories used. The source of the data is well known—the National Sample Surveys of Employment and Unemployment conducted every five years by the National Sample Survey Organization (NSSO) of the Central Statistical Office (CSO) (Government of India). We choose to confine attention to the prime-age (15-59 years) persons, who are classified as employed or unemployed on the basis of their Usual Principal Activity Status.[8] The idea is to focus on the employment conditions of the core group of the working population.[9]

We define three main types of employment—regular wage employment, casual wage employment and self-employment. Persons in regular wage employment are those who are engaged on a long-term basis and receive salaries (usually on a monthly basis). Two types of regular wage employees can also be distinguished: formal and informal. Formal regular employees (or simply formal employees) are to be found in the organized sector. They have job security, substantial non-wage benefits, and access to some kind of social security;[10] their wages also happen to be higher than the labour incomes of all other categories of workers.[11] Persons engaged in casual wage employment are those who are generally hired on a daily basis and paid a daily wage. The category of self-employed workers includes three sub-categories of employed workers—own account workers, unpaid family workers and employers. Own account workers are those who run their own household enterprises without hiring labour on a regular basis. Unpaid family workers are members of the own account workers' households who work in the household enterprises and share in the incomes derived from these enterprises. Employers are own account workers who hire labour on a regular basis to run their enterprises.[12]

The two main sectors of India's dualistic economy—organized and unorganized—have long-established and generally accepted definitions. The organized sector (which can be taken as equivalent to Lewis's modern sector) includes all government establishments, public sector enterprises, private corporate sector enterprises, and those private non-corporate enterprises that have at least ten regular wage employees. The unorganized sector (which can be taken as equivalent to Lewis's traditional sector) is simply the rest of the economy.

Table 4.1

Average Annual Rate of Growth of Prime-age Persons in Employment and the Labour Force (%)

	1983-1993/94	*1993/94-2004/05*	*1983-2004/05*
Organized Sector Employment	*1.1*	*0.8*	*1.0*
Formal employment	1.1	-0.2	0.4
Informal-regular wage employment	1.1	3.4	2.3
Unorganized Sector Employment	*2.1*	*2.2*	*2.2*
Informal employment (1)	2.1	2.2	2.2
Self-employment	1.6	2.5	2.0
Casual wage employment	2.8	1.1	1.9
Informal-regular wage employment (1)	2.8	5.4	4.2
Self-employment and casual wage employment	2.1	1.9	2.0
Regular wage employment, formal and informal	1.8	2.5	2.1
Total Employment	*2.0*	*2.0*	*2.0*
Labour Force	*2.0*	*2.1*	*2.0*

Note: (1) – inclusive of informal-regular wage employment in the organized sector.
Source: Author's estimates based on data presented in Appendix Table 1.

We can now consider the trends suggested by the data in Table 4.1. A first noteworthy fact is that the employment growth in the economy has been no different from the growth of the labour force. The increased supply of labour, it seems, created its own demand. This, of course, should surprise no one; in an economy where self-employment and casual wage employment overwhelmingly dominate, and there is no institutionalized social protection for the vast majority of the workers, unemployment is an option available only to the well-off.[13] One implication is that the rate of unemployment cannot be taken as an indicator of employment conditions. The other implication is that the observed growth in the number of persons in employment, by itself, tells us very little about the growth of demand for labour in the economy and hence gives us no idea of how the employment conditions have changed. In order to understand the nature of change in employment conditions, we need to see how the different types of employment—self-employment, casual wage employment and regular wage employment (formal and informal)—have grown.

Second, these different types of employment have grown roughly at the same rate over the long run (1983-2004/05). This fact, together with the fact that the labour force was also growing at the very same rate, suggests that simultaneously labour use in the economy increased (we shall come back to the point) and that the employment conditions changed little. Third, employment in the organized sector has grown at a much slower rate than the labour force. This means that much of the incremental labour force has had to find work in the unorganized sector so that the rate of growth of employment in the unorganized sector was higher than that of the labour force in the economy. Fourth, the rate of growth of formal employment was even slower than that of organized sector employment; informal regular wage employment grew rather rapidly in the organized sector. Finally, the growth of informal regular wage employment in the unorganized sector was faster than the growth of total employment.[14] This may be taken as indicating that the nature of employment in the unorganized sector is beginning to change at the margin. It must be noted, however, that the overall growth of regular wage employment (formal and informal taken together) has been no higher than the growth of the labour force in the economy. What has changed is the formal–informal composition of regular wage employment.

Thus, over the long run, the declining share of the organized sector in total employment and the growing informality of organized sector employment (and hence of regular wage employment, in general) were the only noteworthy changes. When the trends during the two sub-periods—1983-1993/94 and 1993/94-2004/05—are compared, another important fact comes to light. It may be noticed that the second sub-period was the period of opening up or globalization of India's economy. The data in Table 4.1 strongly suggest that the opening up of the economy had an adverse effect on the growth of formal employment and a stimulating effect on the growth of informal employment in the organized sector. Even during the period 1983-1993/94, the rate of growth of organized sector employment was slower than that of the labour force, but the growth of informal employment was no higher than that of formal employment. During the second period, the growth of organized sector employment showed significant deceleration (even while output growth accelerated, as we shall see below), formal employment declined in absolute terms, and there was accelerated growth of informal employment.

The data presented in Table 4.2 confirm these observations. Over the long run (that is, between 1983 and 2004/05), the type-structure of employment (considering only the broad types—self-employment, casual wage employment, and regular wage employment) showed near-perfect stability. Hidden beneath this stability were two significant changes: (i) the share of the organized sector in total employment declined quite significantly, and (ii) the share of formal employment in organized sector employment also declined (and this meant a decline in the share of formal regular wage employment in total regular wage employment). Moreover, when the sub-periods are considered, it becomes clear that the opening up of the economy intensified the first trend and generated the second.

Table 4.2

Percentage Distribution of Prime-age Persons in Employment by Type of Employment

	1983	*1993-94*	*2004-05*
Organized Sector Employment	*13.6*	*12.4*	*10.9*
Formal employment	10.2	9.2	7.3
Informal employment	3.4	3.2	3.6
Unorganized Sector Employment	*86.4*	*87.6*	*89.1*
Informal employment (1)	89.8	90.8	92.7
Self-employment	52.3	50.0	52.4
Casual wage employment	31.6	34.3	31.1
Regular wage employment (1)	5.9	6.5	9.2
Self-employment and casual wage employment	83.9	84.3	83.5
Regular wage employment, formal and informal	16.1	15.7	16.5

Note: (1) – inclusive of informal regular wage employment in the organized sector.

Source: Author's estimates based on data presented in Appendix Table 1.

The data in Table 4.2 also highlight two additional features of employment in India. First, they show how small the share of the organized sector in total employment was even in the early 1980s. And, of course, this share became progressively smaller over time. In 2004-05, just about 11 per cent of India's employed workers were in the organized sector of the economy. And not all of them were in formal employment, that is, employment that offers not just relatively a high wage but also non-wage benefits and some measure of social protection. Only about 67 per cent of the organized sector employees (accounting for just 7 per cent of India's employed workers) were engaged in formal employment in 2004-05. Second, the data show the overwhelming dominance of the traditional forms of employment—self-employment and casual wage employment. In 2004-05, 84 per cent of India's workers worked either as self-employed or as casual labourers. And this percentage had remained stable over the long period 1983-2004/05.

India's employment conditions, therefore, have been deteriorating in one important respect: the degree of formality of employment has been declining. In some other respects, however, the employment conditions have been improving, even if marginally.

Table 4.3

Unemployment and Underemployment of Prime-age Persons in the Labour Force

	1983	*1993-94*	*2004-05*
Rate (%) of Unemployment	3.2	2.9	3.5
Days of employment per week of:			
Persons in self- and casual employment	5.32	5.41	5.36
Persons in self-employment	5.7	5.7	5.7
Persons in casual wage employment	4.7	5.0	4.8
Rate (%) of Underemployment of:			
Persons in self- and casual employment	11.3	9.8	10.7
Persons in self-employment	5.0	5.0	5.0
Persons in casual wage employment	21.7	16.7	20.0

Note: The estimates of the number of days of employment per week are derived by using data on daily activity status (activity status on each half-day of the week preceding the date of survey) of the prime-age persons in employment, according to usual principal status. The rates of underemployment are worked out by supposing that all workers would have worked six days in a week had work been available.

Source: Author's estimates based on data available from 38th, 50th and 61st Rounds of the National Sample Survey of Employment and Unemployment.

The data in Table 4.3 show three things. First, the rate of unemployment showed no trend. This, of course, is not a new finding; it is a straightforward implication of the observed equality between the rate of growth of persons in employment and that of persons in the labour force. Second, while underemployment is significant for both the self-employed and the casual wage employed, it is obviously far more serious for the latter. Third, the rate of underemployment of the workers in self-employment and casual wage employment showed some fluctuations but no systematic trend.

To come back to a point noted earlier, labour use in the economy certainly increased; indeed, it grew at roughly the same pace as the labour force. This follows from the facts that the rate of unemployment remained stable at a very low level and that the rate of underemployment declined only very slightly.

Interestingly, notwithstanding the strong trend toward informality and the absence of any kind of tightness in labour markets, real wages increased for all types of employees (Table 4.4). Indeed, the real wages actually increased faster during the period of globalization than during the earlier period. Thus, the average real wage per day for casual labour increased at 1.6 per cent per annum during the period 1983-1993/94 and at 2.5 per cent per annum during the period 1993/94-2004/05. And the average real wage per day for regular employees (both formal and informal) increased at a rate of 2.8 per cent per annum during the period 1983-1993/94 and at 3.1 per cent per annum during the period 1993/94-2004/05.

Table 4.4

Daily Real Wage (in Rs. at 2004-05 prices)
of Prime-age Persons in Wage Employment

	1983	*1993/94*	*2004/05*
Regular wage employees	*91*	*122*	*170*
Formal	...	...	288
Informal	...	...	91
Casual wage employees	33	39	*51*

Source: Author's estimates based on data available from 38th, 50th and 61st Rounds of National Sample Survey of Employment and Unemployment.

All this may seem rather puzzling to those who regard wage as the variable that brings demand for and supply of labour into equilibrium. But wages in India are not, and cannot be, determined through demand–supply equilibrium. For the organized sector, which pays a wage that is substantially higher than the average labour income in the unorganized sector, the supply of labour is 'unlimited' (since most of the unorganized sector workers would obviously prefer to work in the organized sector). In the unorganized sector, casual wage employment is the overwhelmingly dominant form of wage employment and this allows work-sharing, which is what is reflected in the high level of underemployment confronted by the casual employees. So, there is excess supply of wage labour in both the organized and unorganized sectors. Thus, wages in both sectors are and must be exogenously given. In the organized sector, state regulations and collective bargaining determine the wage rate (as also the non-wage benefits). In the unorganized sector, the wage rate for casual labour is governed by the labour income in self-employment and hence ultimately by labour productivity in household enterprises.[15]

It must be noticed that the average real wage of regular wage employees increased faster than the average real wage of casual wage employees during both periods. Thus, wage inequality was clearly growing. However, the extent to which the growth of the average real wage of regular wage employees reflected the growth of the average wage of the formal regular employees cannot be discerned for lack of data. The data for the year 2004/05 show that the wage gap between formal regular employees and informal regular employees is much larger than the wage gap between informal regular employees and casual employees. Given the pattern of growth of the different categories of wage employees (as discussed above), it can be plausibly hypothesized that it is mainly the wage gap between the formal regular employees and the informal regular employees that has grown. But more evidence is clearly required to get beyond hypothesizing.

It is important to recognize that the gap in wage income over a period (a week or a month or a year) between regular wage employees and casual wage employees is larger than the gap in wage per day; the regular employees work for a significantly larger number of days than the casual employees over any given period. Besides, since the rate of underemployment has declined for the informal regular employees, while it has remained basically unchanged for the casual employees, the gap in wage income over a period has clearly increased significantly more than the gap in the wage per day.

What remains unseen in all this is the average labour income of the self-employed. But this, as argued above, bears a direct relationship with the average wage income of the casual employees. Given that the average wage income of the casual employees has been growing, we can suppose that the average labour income of the self-employed must have been increasing too. Some supporting evidence comes from estimates of mixed income per self-employed person.[16] These estimates show that the mixed income per self-employed increased at the rate of 1.6 per cent per annum during the period 1983-93/94 and at 2.4 per cent per annum during the period 1993/94-2004/05. These are very close to the rates of growth of the casual wage rate over the same period. Indirect evidence is also available from estimates of incidence of poverty for the different categories of workers (Table 4.5). These estimates show that the incidence of poverty has always been and remains the highest among the casual wage employees and lowest among the regular wage employees; the incidence of poverty among the self-employed is lower than that among the casual employees but higher than that among the regular employees. Obviously, the average labour income of the self-employed is much lower than the average wage income of the regular employees. On the other hand, it is not implausible to assume rough equality between the average labour income of the self-employed and the average wage income of the casual employees. The average income of the self-employed, of course, includes not just labour income but also rent and profit, and is hence substantially higher than the average labour income, which is what equals the average wage income of the casual employees. Given such relationships, the declining incidence of poverty among the self-employed reflects rising labour income just as the declining incidence of poverty among the casual employees reflects rising wage income.

Table 4.5

Incidence of Poverty (%) among Prime-age Persons in Employment

	1983	*1993/94*	*2004/05*
Regular wage employees	38.0	24.4	17.8
Formal	...	...	6.0
Informal	...	...	26.9
Casual wage employees	76.7	69.1	56.4
Self-employed	57.4	47.8	36.3
All employed	60.4	51.4	39.5

Note: The incidence of poverty is the percentage of persons in the households of the workers concerned that have a per capita expenditure below the poverty line. The poverty lines used are those recently adopted by the Planning Commission: Rs. 446.7 for rural inhabitants and Rs. 578.8 for urban inhabitants, both at 2004-05 prices.

Source: Author's estimates based on data available from the 38th, 50th and 61st Rounds of the National Sample Survey of Employment and Unemployment.

Thus, the rapid and accelerating economic growth that occurred during the period 1983-2004/05 wholly failed to set in motion a process of labour transfer from the unorganized to the organized sector but increased labour incomes across the board and thus reduced poverty. The latter phenomenon is explained by the growth of output per worker in both the organized and the unorganized sectors.

As can be seen from Table 4.6, the Net Domestic Product (NDP) grew at a rate of 5.5 per cent per annum during the period 1983-1993/94 and at 6.9 per cent per annum during the period 1993/94-2004/05.[17] Growth acceleration occurred in both the organized and unorganized sectors though the organized sector recorded faster growth during both the sub-periods. Moreover, the growth of the unorganized sector was fairly rapid during both sub-periods, which meant decent growth of output per worker. It is this growth of output per worker that translated into increased labour incomes for both the self-employed and the casual wage employees, and hence reduced poverty. The faster growth of labour incomes for all types of workers during the second sub-period is also not surprising in view of the faster growth of output per worker in both the organized and unorganized sectors.

Table 4.6

Net Domestic Product (at 2004-05 Prices): Average Annual Rate of Growth (%)

	1983-1993/94	*1993/94-2004/05*	*1983-2004/05*
Net Domestic Product (NDP)			
Aggregate	5.5	6.9	6.2
Organized sector	6.2	7.8	7.0
Unorganized sector	5.1	6.3	5.7
NDP per Employed Worker			
Aggregate	3.5	4.9	4.2
Organized sector	5.1	7.0	6.0
Unorganized sector	3.0	4.1	3.5

Note: The growth rates are estimated by using the compound interest formula on initial and terminal values.

Source: Author's estimates based on data from National Accounts Statistics and National Sample Survey of Employment and Unemployment.

The growth of output per worker was, of course, much faster in the organized sector than in the unorganized sector during both the sub-periods. And the gap in output per worker between the sectors increased faster during the second sub-period. Thus, dualism was becoming stronger (the gap in labour income per worker between the sectors was widening, leading to a rise in income inequality in the economy) and globalization of the economy intensified the tendency.

The growth of the organized sector, it should be noticed, was relatively jobless and productivity-led during both the sub-periods, but more so during the second than the first sub-period. The employment elasticity was low (0.18) during the period 1983-1993/94 and even lower (0.10) during the period 1993/94-2004/05. The rate of growth of the average real wage of regular wage employees was much slower than the rate of growth of output per worker in the organized sector during both sub-periods. And the gap between the two rates widened particularly sharply during the second sub-period. It thus appears that the relatively jobless, productivity-led growth increased the share of profits in the organized sector's value added and that the opening up of the economy considerably strengthened this trend.[18] This trend contributed to the growth of income inequality in the economy.

It is not easy to draw any unambiguous conclusion about whether or not the employment conditions improved overall. On the one hand, the share of 'good' jobs—jobs that offer not just relatively high wage but also substantial non-wage benefits including social protection—in total employment declined; employment conditions can be said to have deteriorated on this account. On the other hand, labour use in the economy increased *pari passu* with labour force growth; absorption of incremental labour force was associated with stable levels of underemployment and unemployment. Labour productivity also recorded decent growth so that labour incomes increased for all categories of workers and the incidence of poverty generally declined. Employment conditions can be said to have improved on these accounts. At the same time, the gaps in labour productivity and in labour income between the organized and unorganized sectors were widening. Such strengthening of dualism must count as deterioration of employment conditions.

Social Protection: The Concerns, the Initiatives and the Issues

India's development experience shows why social protection has emerged as a major concern in recent years. Rapid economic growth was associated with a declining proportion of workers with formal employment and thus with a declining proportion of population with access to formal social protection. And though the declining incidence of poverty meant a declining proportion of the population in desperate need of social assistance, the proportion remains large.

India's experience also shows why a two-pronged approach to developing a social protection system is required. If economic growth continues to fail to increase the proportion of population with access to formal social protection, any objective of making access to formal social protection universal in the long run looks wholly utopian. It is important, therefore, to look into the possibility of modifying the growth process so as to ensure that formal employment grows faster than the labour force. On the other hand, even if this is achieved and even if poverty continues to decline, the proportion of the population in desperate need of social assistance would remain substantial for quite a long time to come. It is, therefore, essential to put into place a minimum level of social protection for the poor and the vulnerable here and now.

For workers in poor jobs, social protection has to mean more than just social security and has to incorporate two elements. The first element relates to social assistance meant to ameliorate persistent deprivation (low nutritional, health and educational status, poor housing and sanitation, etc.) associated with poverty, which arises from inadequate and low-productivity (hence low-income) employment. The second relates to what is commonly understood as social security, that is, safety nets that help the poor and the vulnerable to meet contingencies such as illness, accident, death and old age.

It has to be said that the need for social protection of the unorganized workers in poor jobs has been recognized for quite some time in India.[19] But a coherent policy response was missing. There existed a patchwork of programmes, with varying but generally minuscule degree of coverage, run by the Central Government, the state governments and Non-governmental

Organizations (NGOs). These included social assistance programmes (including special employment schemes, food and nutrition programmes, and programmes for housing, education and healthcare), welfare funds for particular groups of unorganized workers, and a variety of micro-insurance schemes.[20]

Major initiatives for the establishment of a comprehensive system of social protection for all workers in poor jobs have come only in recent years. Three recent initiatives recognize a defined minimum level of social protection as a right of workers and the delivery of such protection as an obligation of the government. The first—the Mahatma Gandhi National Rural Employment Guarantee Act (MGNREGA), 2005—is concerned with social assistance for poor workers delivered through the provision of a guaranteed minimum quantity of wage employment at a decent minimum wage. The second—the Unorganized Workers' Social Security Act (UWSSA), 2008—is concerned with safety nets for poor workers against contingencies delivered through the implementation of a number of special insurance schemes. The third—a proposed Food Security Act (FSA)—is again concerned with social assistance delivered through the supply of a minimum quantity of basic food grains at highly subsidized prices.

Under the MGNREGA, a special employment scheme (the Mahatma Gandhi National Rural Employment Scheme or MGNREGS), which guarantees up to 100 days of employment to rural households at a specified minimum wage, has been implemented in all rural areas of the country since 2008.[21] Under the UWSSA, special insurance schemes for providing life and disability cover, health and maternity benefits and old age pension to unorganized workers with below-poverty-line (BPL) incomes are beginning to be implemented.[22] Under these schemes, the Government would pay the required premiums and the designated beneficiaries would not have to pay anything. The FSA (currently under discussion) proposes guaranteed entitlements of subsidized foodgrains for 75 per cent of the country's population (covering 90 per cent of the rural population and 50 per cent of the urban population) that is judged to be poor and vulnerable.[23]

It will be some time before we can properly evaluate the effectiveness of these programmes in delivering social protection to workers in poor jobs.[24] Meanwhile, there are at least three issues that are still being debated and the outcomes of these debates will have a bearing on the shape of the programmes in future. First, how do we define an appropriate minimum level of social protection? Presently, the programmes are geared towards ensuring a poverty-line income and towards minimizing the probability of contingencies driving the actual incomes below the poverty-line income. It is arguable, however, that the poverty-line income, as currently defined, only allows an exit from extreme poverty; protecting this income, therefore, is simply not good enough. On the other hand, it is not clear that programmes seeking to protect higher-than-poverty-line income are fiscally sustainable. A second issue concerns the question as to whether these programmes should be universal or targeted. We may note that the MGNREGS is universal in coverage but effectively targets the poor by offering only casual wage employment involving manual labour. The schemes under UWSSA, on the other hand, are targeted on below-poverty-line population. It can be argued that identifying the poor on the ground is a hugely difficult task and the targeted programmes could easily fail to reach a section of the poor while benefiting a section of the non-poor. The proposed FSA is also conceived as a targeted programme and could encounter the same difficulties as the UWSSA. A third issue relates to the question of the relative effectiveness of the direct delivery of goods and services versus cash transfers. Direct delivery of goods and services to the poor can be administratively very difficult and costly. Cash transfers, on the other hand, create a demand for goods and services but do nothing to increase the supply. For cash transfers to work, therefore, the supply of the relevant goods and services must be perfectly elastic, that is, there must be large excess capacity in the production of these goods and services. Or else they would generate inflation and no benefits for the poor.

Concluding Observations

For a long time, employment and social protection were not considered as independent objectives of development policy; the growth of the organized sector was expected to deliver both to a growing proportion of the labour force in labour-surplus dual economies. The maximization of growth of the organized sector was, therefore, viewed as the central objective of development policy. In achieving this objective, development policy has been remarkably successful in a significant number of countries. However, the growth of the organized sector persistently failed to deliver good jobs and social protection to a growing proportion of the labour force.

This experience has underlined the need to view employment and social protection as independent objectives of development policy. At the same time, however, globalization has made these objectives more daunting. The emergence of global production systems dominated by multinationals and the vastly increased competition from imports faced by domestic producers have generated strong pressures for the adoption of capital- and skill-intensive technologies, thereby undermining the capacity of governments to influence the employment intensity of growth in the organized sector. Globalization has also increased economic instability worldwide and has thereby increased the exposure of workers in developing countries to risks of economic adversity.

Hardly any effort has so far been made to increase the employment intensity of growth in the organized sector. On the other hand, efforts are now being made in quite a few developing countries to provide a minimum level of social protection to workers in the unorganized sector. But these efforts are at best tentative. It is widely recognized that delivering social protection to workers in the unorganized sector really means delivering transfer incomes. But this recognition immediately brings into focus certain questions that remain to be satisfactorily answered. Some of these have already been noted: How is a minimum level of social protection to be defined? Should 'minimum social protection' programmes be targeted or universal in coverage? Would cash transfers do or would real goods and services need to be directly supplied?

However, there are other weightier questions to be answered. To what extent are social protection programmes fiscally sustainable? Could the allocation of substantial resources to social protection programmes lower the growth of the organized sector? Or could social protection, by lowering risk-aversion, release the entrepreneurial energies of the unorganized sector workers and hence stimulate growth?

Much thinking remains to be done.

References

Ahluwalia, M.S. (2002). "Economic Reforms in India since 1991: Has Gradualism Worked?", *Journal of Economic Perspectives* 16(3): 67-88.

Ghose, Ajit K. (2010). "Reinventing Development Economics", *Economic and Political Weekly* 45(42): 41-50.

——— (2011a). "India's MGNREGS: Will It Reduce Poverty and Stimulate Growth?", Paper prepared for the Employment and Labour Market Analysis Department. Geneva: International Labour Office.

——— (2011b). "Work in India", (*Mimeo*). New Delhi: Institute for Human Development.

Ghose, Ajit K., N. Majid and C. Ernst (2008). *The Global Employment Challenge*. Geneva: International Labour Organization (ILO).

International Labour Organization (ILO) (2010). *World Social Security Report*. Geneva.

Joshi, V. and I.M.D. Little (1994). *India: Macroeconomics and Political Economy*. Washington, D.C.: World Bank.

——— (1996). *India's Economic Reforms*. Oxford: Clarendon Press.

Kannan, K.P. (2009). "Social Security for Workers", (*Mimeo*). New Delhi: Institute for Human Development.

Kochar, K., U. Kumar, R. Rajan, A. Subramanian and I. Tokatlidis (2006). "India's Pattern of Development: What Happened, What Follows", *Journal of Monetary Economics* 53(5): 981-1019.

Mahendra Dev, S. (2010). "Social Protection in India: Issues and Concerns", Paper presented at the *International Consultation on Human Development in India* (New Delhi, 5-6 February 2010) organized by the Institute for Human Development (New Delhi), Indian Council for Social Science Research (New Delhi) and the World Bank.

National Commission for Enterprises in the Unorganized Sector (NCEUS), Government of India (2006). *Social Security for Unorganized Workers: Report*. New Delhi.

Srinivasan, T.N. and S. Tendulkar (2003). *Reintegrating India with the World Economy*. Washington, D.C.: Institute for International Economics.

Notes

1. Developing economies are dual economies with surplus labour. A dual economy has two distinct sectors—an organized or formal or modern sector and an unorganized or informal or traditional sector. Surplus labour exists in the form of underemployment of the workers in self-employment and casual wage employment in the unorganized sector. For a detailed discussion of these features, see Ghose (2010).
2. This should have been recognized as such, for it was not difficult to see that given the initial conditions and the rather high growth of labour force in developing countries, the growth of the organized sector had to be absurdly high for there to be transfer of workers from the unorganized to the organized sector. The point is discussed in some detail in Ghose (2010).
3. Note, however, that the growth of labour productivity in the unorganized sector resulted essentially from output growth, which had much to do with the growth of demand in the organized sector for the products of the unorganized sector. Spillover effects through labour transfers were rare. See Ghose, *et al.* (2008) for evidence from a set of developing countries.

4. Recent estimates (ILO, 2010) suggest that 80 per cent of the world's population lacks access to formal social protection. If correct, this would imply that more than 90 per cent of the population of the developing world lacks access to formal social protection.
5. Contributory social insurance schemes are clearly irrelevant. Providing social protection to workers in poor jobs of various types means providing transfer incomes, which may, of course, be disbursed through special employment schemes.
6. A number of studies discuss the reforms implemented in the 1980s and in the 1990s. See, for example, Joshi and Little (1994; 1996); Ahluwalia (2002); Srinivasan and Tendulkar (2003); and Kochar *et al.* (2006).
7. Some data from the most recent survey covering the period 2009/10 have just become available, but these data need to be subjected to a proper scrutiny before they can be used in analyses. A quick look suggests that their inclusion would not alter the trends identified for the period 1983-2004/05.
8. Usual Principal Activity Status of a person is the activity—employment, unemployment and non-participation in the labour force—in which he/she was engaged for the major part of the year preceding the date of the survey.
9. We are leaving out child workers, elderly workers and those prime-age persons who are in employment according to Usual Subsidiary Activity Status (which refers to the activity—employment, unemployment and non-participation in the labour force – in which a person was engaged for only a minor part of the year preceding the date of the survey). Any improvement of employment conditions of the prime-age workers (according to Usual Principal Activity Status) would arguably lower the labour force participation of these other types of workers.
10. For an account of the kind of social security available to the formal employees, see Kannan (2009).
11. The level of wage, it should be noted, has not been used as a criterion for classification.
12. It needs to be said that workers in India often engage in more than one type of employment during any given period. The categorization of employed persons described above is based on what is called 'the major time criterion'. A person is regarded as employed if he/she has been engaged in economically gainful activities for the major part of the reference year, and as unemployed if he/she has not been engaged in economically gainful activities for the major part of the reference year but was looking or available for engagement. A person identified as employed is assigned to a particular category if he/she has been in that type of employment for the major part of the period of his/her employment.
13. Ghose (2011b) elaborates on the point and provides some supporting evidence.
14. It can be checked from the data in Appendix Table 1 that, over the period 1983-2004/05, informal-regular wage employment in the unorganized sector grew at a rate of 6 per cent per annum while total employment in the sector grew at a rate of 2.2 per cent per annum.
15. For elaboration of the arguments, see Ghose (2011b).
16. These estimates are derived by combining the data on mixed income in the unorganized sector, available from National Accounts Statistics, and the data on persons in self-employment, available from the National Sample Surveys of Employment and Unemployment (presented in Appendix A-4.1).
17. We are considering NDP rather than GDP here because data on NDP are also available for the organized and unorganized sectors separately. The average annual growth rates of GDP (estimated by using the compound interest formula on initial and

terminal values) were: 1983-1993/94: 5.1 per cent, 1993/94-2004/05: 6.3 per cent, and 1983-2004/05: 5.7 per cent.

18. The share of 'operating surplus' in NDP of the organized sector increased from 30.6 per cent in 1983 to 41.0 per cent in 1993/94 and further to 45.8 per cent in 2004/05.
19. The Report of the National Commission on Rural Labour (established by the Government of India in 1991) discussed the issue of social security for rural workers in detail and made a whole set of recommendations.
20. For comprehensive reviews of these programmes, see NCEUS (2006); Kannan (2009); and Mahendra Dev (2010).
21. A detailed description of the scheme is available in Ghose (2011a).
22. A detailed description of the schemes is available in Kannan (2009).
23. The below-poverty-line (BPL) persons (comprising 46 per cent of rural inhabitants and 28 per cent of urban inhabitants in 2004/05) are to be given entitlement to 7 kgs of foodgrains per person per month at highly subsidized prices while the above-poverty-line (APL) but vulnerable persons (comprising 44 per cent of rural inhabitants and 22 per cent of urban inhabitants in 2004/05) are to be given entitlement to 4 kgs of foodgrains per person per month at less highly subsidized prices. Provisions are also to be made for running feeding programmes for children, pregnant and nursing mothers, and destitute and vulnerable groups.
24. A recent study suggests that though MGNREGS has substantially increased the money incomes of the rural poor, it has thus far failed to reduce poverty because the government has done precious little to increase the food supply in the country. See Ghose (2011a).

Appendix A-4.1

Prime-age Persons (in millions) in Employment and the Labour Force

	1983	*1993-94*	*2004-05*
Employment	*238.0*	*293.3*	*365.4*
In Organized Sector	32.4	36.3	39.8
Formal employment	24.2	27.1	26.5
Informal regular wage employment	8.2	9.2	13.3
In Unorganized Sector	205.6	257.0	325.6
Informal employment	*213.8*	*266.2*	*338.9*
Self-employment	124.5	146.7	191.5
Casual wage employment	75.2	100.6	113.6
Informal regular wage employment	14.1	18.9	33.8
Unemployment	*8.0*	*8.7*	*13.2*
Labour force	*246.0*	*302.0*	*378.6*

Note: Prime-age persons are persons in the age group 15-59 years. Employment is employment according to the Usual Principal Status (a person is in employment if he/she has worked for a major part of the year preceding the date of survey). Formal employment is defined as regular wage employment with social protection in the organized sector (all public and private corporate sector establishments and those private establishments outside the corporate sector that employ at least 10 workers). Wage employment without social protection in the organized sector is regarded as informal employment. And all employment outside the organized sector is regarded as informal. The direct estimate of formal employment could be derived from the National Sample Survey (NSS) data only for 2004-05. This turned out to be close to the estimate of organized sector employment made by the Ministry of Labour and Employment (these estimates are published annually). We assume, on this basis, that the estimates made by the Ministry of Labour and Employment are really estimates of formal employment and not of organized sector employment. So the estimates of formal employment presented above are the estimates made by the Ministry of Labour and Employment. Direct estimates of informal employment in the organized sector could also be derived only for 2004-05; the estimates for other years are derived by using the known fact that the share of informal employment in organized sector employment increased, particular after 1993-94. It should be added (for the sake of clarity) that while informal employment in the organized sector includes regular wage employment as well as casual wage employment, informal employment in the unorganized sector includes regular wage employment, casual wage employment and self-employment.

Source: National Sample Survey (38th, 50th and 61st Rounds) and Ministry of Labour and Employment.

5 Labour Demand Trends, Inequality and Social Protection in South Africa

An Overview

Haroon Bhorat, Natasha Mayet and Carlene van der Westhuizen

Introduction

South Africa's formal transition from White minority rule in 1994 justifiably received international attention and acclaim. In April 1994, the country's first democratically elected party, the African National Congress (ANC), was voted into power. Masked by this relatively peaceful transition from apartheid, however, was the challenge that lay ahead in terms of dealing with the economic vestiges of the system of racial exclusivity. Nowhere is this challenge more apparent than in the labour market. Using the labour market as an entry point, this paper examines three inter-related areas. Firstly, through an analysis of labour supply trends in South Africa since the onset of democracy, we assess the implications of output, productivity, and trade flows for labour demand trends. Secondly, and in relation to this particular labour demand trajectory in the domestic economy, we illustrate the nature of income inequality in South Africa, at both the individual and household levels. Finally, we argue that the country's social protection system may currently lie at the heart of the anti-inequality measures pursued by the State.

The authors would like to thank Elné Jacobs for her assistance with some of the data preparation for this chapter. We also acknowledge the comments of two anonymous referees.

Employment Creation since 1994: Sectoral Patterns, Employment Elasticities and Trade Flows

We explore below some of the key changes in the post-apartheid labour market in South Africa. The availability of trend data from 1995 to 2009 makes it possible to examine the broad shifts in labour force participation, employment, and unemployment during the last 15 years. We also consider, through the use of a decomposition methodology, the impact of trade flows on labour demand during the first decade of democracy, with the explicit aim of attempting an analysis of how global integration may have impacted the domestic labour market.

Labour Market Trends in South Africa 1995-2009: A Brief Overview

Table 5.1 shows that during the first 15 years of democratic rule in South Africa, the economy generated approximately 3.2 million jobs and

Table 5.1

The South African Labour Force, 1995 to 2009

Category	*1995*	*Q3 2009*	*Change*		*Average Annual Growth 1995-2009*
	'000s	*'000s*	*'000s*	*%*	*%*
Official Definition Estimates					
Employment	9,845	12,884	3,039	30.9	1.9
Unemployment	2,032	4,119	2,087	102.8	5.2
Labour Force	11,676	17,003	5,327	45.6	2.7
Broad Definition Estimates					
Employment	9,845	12,884	3,039	30.9	1.9
Unemployment	4,239	5,751	1,512	35.7	2.2
Labour force	13,883	18,635	4,752	34.2	2.1

Notes: 1. Working age population includes individuals aged between 15 and 65 years old.

2. 1995 data are re-weighted according to the 1996 Census. Data from 2000 onwards have been re-weighted according to the 2001 Census.

3. The expanded (broad) definition of the labour force includes discouraged work seekers.

4. The change in definitions of the broad unemployment rate renders the 2009 estimate incomparable with that of 1995.

5. Growth rates in this table are the compounded annual growth rates and were calculated by using the 1995 and the 2009 estimates.

6. The estimates here employ the 'hybrid labour market definitions' for the OHS and LFS.

Source: OHS 1995; QLFS Quarter 3, 2009 (Statistics South Africa).

employment increased at a significant rate of just under 2 per cent per annum. Over the same period, some 5.2 million individuals entered the labour market in search of jobs, representing a 2.7 per cent annual growth rate in the labour force. Consequently, growth in employment fell short of growth in the labour force, and unemployment grew significantly over the period at an average annual rate of 5.2 per cent, representing an increase in the number of broadly defined unemployed of 2 million.

The rise in the number of unemployed meant that some 15 years after democracy, South Africa's unemployment rate stood at 30.9 per cent (broad definition). This gave the economy, an upper-middle income country according to the World Bank, the dubious distinction of yielding one of the highest unemployment rates in the world. The unemployment rate (broad definition) amongst youth (individuals aged between 15 and 24 years) is even higher, and stood at 56.9 per cent in 2009 (QLFS 2009: 3, Statistics South Africa).

Table 5.2 provides a disaggregated overview of aggregate employment shifts by race, gender and age. The number of employed Africans grew significantly at an average annual rate of 2.6 per cent per annum between 1995 and 2009. The breakdown of employment by gender shows that though both male and female employment increased between 1995 and 2009, female employment grew at twice the rate of male employment (3.1 per cent per annum relative to 1.4 per cent). Indeed, the feminization of employment is a key trend observed in the post-apartheid labour market. Furthermore, the share of youth in employment has fallen significantly by around 1.1 percentage points.

Individuals with the highest levels of education experienced the fastest growth in employment, notably those possessing a Grade 12 (4.3 per cent per annum), a Diploma/Certificate with Grade 12 (3.9 per cent per annum), or a Degree (4.9 per cent per annum) qualification.

The above estimates constitute a strong signal of the skills-biased labour demand shifts that have characterized the post-apartheid period, with higher returns accruing to individuals with a Grade 12 or a tertiary qualification. The estimates serve to provide provisional evidence of one of the key attributes of South Africa's labour market, that amidst extraordinarily high levels of unemployment, there is a clear preference

Table 5.2

Changes in Aggregate Employment in South Africa, 1995 to 2009

Indicator	1995		Q3 2009		
	000s	Share (%)	000s	Share (%)	Average Annual Growth 1995-2009
African	6,211	64.4	8,935	69.5	2.6
Coloured	1,163	12.1	1,510	11.7	1.9
Asian	366	3.8	453	3.4	1.5
White	1,905	19.7	1,986	15.4	0.3
Male	5,860	60.8	7,102	55.1	1.4
Female	3,785	39.2	5,782	44.9	3.1
15-24 years	1,141	11.8	1,373	10.7	1.3
25-34 years	3,330	34.5	4,322	33.5	1.9
35-44 years	2,900	30.1	3,595	27.9	1.5
45-54 years	1,609	16.7	2,504	19.4	3.2
55-65 years	665	6.9	1,090	8.5	3.6
None	782	8.1	442	3.4	-4.0
Incomplete GET	3,064	31.8	2,544	19.7	-1.3
Complete GET	2,120	22.0	3,353	26.0	3.3
Matriculation (Grade 12)	2,131	22.1	3,820	29.7	4.3
Diploma/Certificate, less Grade 12	102	1.1	102	0.8	0.0
Diploma/Certificate, Grade 12	904	9.4	1,553	12.1	3.9
Degree	460	4.8	901	7.0	4.9
Total	**9,845**	**100**	**12,884**	**100**	**1.9**

Notes: 1. Working age population includes individuals aged between 15 and 65 years old.

2. 1995 data are re-weighted according to the 1996 Census. Data from 2000 onwards have been re-weighted according to the 2001 Census.

3. Growth rates in this table are the compounded annual growth rates and were calculated using the 1995 and the 2009 estimates.

4. GET means General Education and Training. The educational categories are No education, Incomplete GET (Grades 0-8), Complete GET (Grades 9-11), Matriculation (Grade 12), a Diploma/Certificate without completed Matriculation, a Diploma/Certificate with completed Matriculation, and a Degree from a university.

5. Shares in total employment may not add up to 100 since 'Other' and 'Unspecified' categories are not shown in the table.

Source: OHS 1995; QLFS Quarter 3, 2009 (Statistics South Africa).

for skilled over unskilled workers amongst employers. This is a theme we return to in greater detail below.

Employment Dynamics by Sector and Occupation

Employment growth since 1995 has been unevenly distributed among the different sectors, with most growth occurring in the tertiary sector (Table 5.3). Tertiary employment grew by almost 3.3 million, representing 96 per cent of the change in employment during the given period. When these data are analysed at the three-digit SIC level, the key result is that employment growth in post-apartheid South Africa has been driven by the financial and business services sector on the one hand, and the wholesale and retail trade sector on the other hand. The latter, wherein the informal sector is dominant, has thus been a key generator of jobs within the domestic economy. The data show that these two main sectors alone accounted for close to 2.2 million of the 3 million new jobs created in South Africa between 1995 and 2009. Put differently, 66 per cent of all employment generation in post-apartheid South Africa can be located within these two sectors. On the other hand, primary sector employment, specifically agriculture and mining, experienced a significant decline in employment of 17.3 per cent and 4.4 per cent per annum, respectively.

The secondary sectors also experienced employment expansion over the 15-year period, with manufacturing and construction adding approximately 271,000 and 608,000 jobs, respectively. The relatively poor performance of manufacturing reflects both lost opportunities since the 1960s and the sector's ongoing lack of dynamism and global competitiveness in the post-1994 era. We turn, in greater detail below, to an analysis of the relationship between this global competitiveness and employment.

As the results presented in Figure 5.1 indicate, of the close to 1.1 million jobs generated in the financial and business services sector, about 900,000 emanated from the 'Other' sub-category, which includes mainly the activities of employment agencies, labour brokers and security services. This result suggests that job growth within the financial and business services main sector has effectively been driven by the rapid rise of security services and temporary employment services.

Table 5.3

Sectoral Distribution of Employment Change

Sector	1995		Q3 2009		AAG	Change	
	'000s	Share (%)	'000s	Share (%)	1995 to 2009	'000s	Share (%)
Primary	1,696	17.9	952	7.4	-4.0	-744	-22
Agriculture	1,247	13.2	653	5.1	-4.5	-594	-17.3
Mining	449	4.8	299	2.3	-2.9	-150	-4.4
Secondary	1,988	21.0	2,861	22.2	2.8	873	25
Manufacturing	1,452	15.4	1,723	13.4	1.2	271	7.9
Utilities	86	0.9	81	0.6	-0.5	-5	-0.2
Construction	449	4.8	1,057	8.2	6.3	608	17.7
Tertiary	5,774	61.0	9,064	70.4	3.3	3,290	96
Wholesale and Retail	1,684	17.8	2,852	22.1	3.8	1,168	34.1
Transport	483	5.1	737	5.7	3.1	254	7.4
Finance	592	6.3	1,682	13.1	7.7	1,090	31.8
CSP	2,205	23.3	2,627	20.4	1.3	422	12.3
Private Household	809	8.6	1,166	9.1	2.6	357	10.4
Total	9,845	100	12,884	100	1.9	3,038	100

Notes: 1. AAG is the average annualized growth rate. Growth rates in this table are the compounded annual growth rates and were calculated using the 1995 and the 2009 estimates.

2. Other and unspecified categories are not shown here.

3. CSP refers to the Community, Social and Personal Services sector.

Source: OHS 1995; QLFS Quarter 3, 2009 (Statistics South Africa).

This is a critical result, as it suggests, on the one hand, that the high incidence of crime in South Africa has, in fact, resulted in a rapid employment expansion within the sub-sector providing crime prevention services. In addition, the rise in the use of employment agencies, for long noted in public debates in South Africa, is now powerfully evident in these numbers. This is also a key result, as it suggests that one of the drivers of employment growth in South Africa since 1994 has, in fact, occurred within non-standard employment across a variety of occupations and sectors. The search for non-permanent employees is, therefore, a strong characteristic of labour demand trends since 1994.

Having examined the sectoral breakdown of employment, we now examine the changes in the occupational and skills composition of

Figure 5.1

Change in Employment, 1995-2009: Financial and Business Services, by Sub-sector

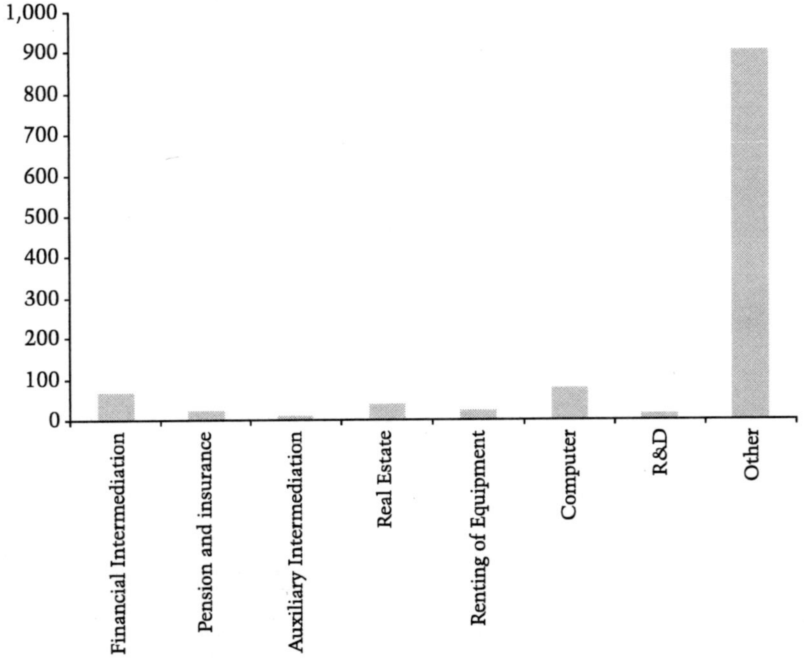

Source: OHS 1995; OHS 1997; LFS September 2000-2007; QLFS Quarter 1-4, 2008 and Quarter 1-3, 2009 (Statistics South Africa).

employment during the period 1995 to 2009 (Table 5.4). Employment growth was positive for all occupational categories, with the exception of domestic workers, whose numbers in employment declined significantly at 8 per cent per annum during the given period. Whilst employment growth was positive at all levels of skills, skilled and semi-skilled employment grew faster than unskilled employment, with skilled and semi-skilled employment growing at the fastest rates (5.2 per cent and 3.8 per cent per annum, respectively) during the period. The share of skilled employment increased significantly by almost 5 percentage points over the period.

Table 5.4

Changes in Occupational Structure of Employment, 1995 to 2009

Occupation	*1995*		*Q3 2009*		*AAG 1995-2009*
	000s	*Share*	*000s*	*Share*	
Managers	508	5.2%	994	7.7%	4.9%
Professionals	331	3.4%	703	5.5%	5.5%
Technicians	1,080	11.0%	1,492	11.6%	2.3%
Clerks	1,155	11.7%	1,431	11.1%	1.5%
Service and Sales Workers	1,092	11.1%	1,792	13.9%	3.6%
Craft and Trade Workers	117	1.2%	1,568	12.2%	20.4%
Operators and Assemblers	1,131	11.5%	1,097	8.5%	-0.2%
Elementary Occupations	1,119	11.4%	2,812	21.8%	6.8%
Domestic Workers	2,984	30.3%	924	7.2%	-8.0%
Skilled	839	8.5%	1,697	13.2%	5.2%
Semi-Skilled	3,496	35.5%	5,888	45.7%	3.8%
Unskilled	4,103	41.7%	3,736	29.0%	-0.7%
Total	**9,845**	**100%**	**12,884**	**100%**	**2.1%**

Notes: 1. Growth rates in this table are the compounded annual growth rates and were calculated using the 1995 and the 2009 estimates.

2. The occupational shares and shares by skill level do not add up to 100 per cent for 1995 and 2001 since the 'unspecified' category in the occupations is not shown in the table. For the 2009 data, the occupational codes did not include an 'unspecified' category for the employed.

3. Skilled occupations include Managers, Professionals and Technicians; unskilled occupations are Elementary and Domestic Workers; the rest are classified here as Semi-skilled.

4. Shares in total employment may not add up to 100 per cent since 'Other' and 'Unspecified' categories are not shown in the table.

Source: OHS 1995; LFS September 2001; QLFS Quarter 3, 2009 (Statistics South Africa).

High annual growth rates in employment were registered by managers and professionals (4.9 per cent and 5.5 per cent per annum, respectively), whose shares in employment also increased significantly during this period. Significant employment expansion also occurred for technicians, clerks, service and sales workers, crafts and trade workers, and elementary workers between 1995 and 2009.

Ultimately then, our detailed, somewhat turgid analysis above of employment shifts for the 15-year period, 1995 to 2009, suggests that a certain number of key, and unique, trends have emerged. Firstly, whilst the economy has created over 3.2 million jobs since 1995, this has been insufficient relative to the number of new work-seekers who have entered the labour market in search of jobs. The consequence has been an increase in the number of narrowly unemployed by over 1.2 million workers. Secondly, in terms of individual characteristics, our data suggest a rise in both the share and growth rate of Africans in total employment. The key result here though, has been a fairly rapid feminization of the workforce, as women's employment rose by close to double that of men's. Thirdly, our education sector results suggest that the South African growth trajectory since 1994 has created employment disproportionately for the better educated and skilled. Fourthly, our sectoral results allude to a key outcome, namely that the vast majority of jobs since 1995 have been created in the financial and business services sector (and to some extent, construction) and the unskilled-intensive wholesale and retail trade sector (notably including the informal sector), whilst shedding large swathes of jobs in the primary sectors. Within the financial and business services sector, however, it has been the rapid rise in crime prevention services and employment agencies that have driven employment, not only in this sector, but in the aggregate as well. Finally, these results are confirmed in our occupational estimates, which suggest skills-biased employment growth.

Employment and Output

Figure 5.2 shows that all sectors in the economy, barring three, experienced growth in both Gross Value Added (GVA) and employment over the period 1995 to 2009. Only three sectors in South Africa saw declining employment between 1995 and 2009, namely agriculture, mining and the utilities sector. GVA growth, on the other hand, was positive across all sectors, barring mining, which experienced a contraction of 0.6 per cent in GVA per annum since 1995. At the same time, the GVA per worker has risen in six of the nine sectors, namely manufacturing, transport, electricity, agriculture, mining and community, social and personal services (CSPs). In other words, the growth in GVA in these sectors was faster than growth in employment, and hence these sectors are found below the 45-degree line in the graph. In the finance sector, GVA per worker has fallen as employment growth was faster than the growth in GVA (7.7 per cent and 5.3 per cent per annum, respectively). In the retail and the construction sectors, GVA growth was roughly proportional to growth in employment, or in other words, GVA per worker was unchanged over the period.

Figure 5.2

Gross Value Added and Employment Growth by Sector, 1995 to 2009

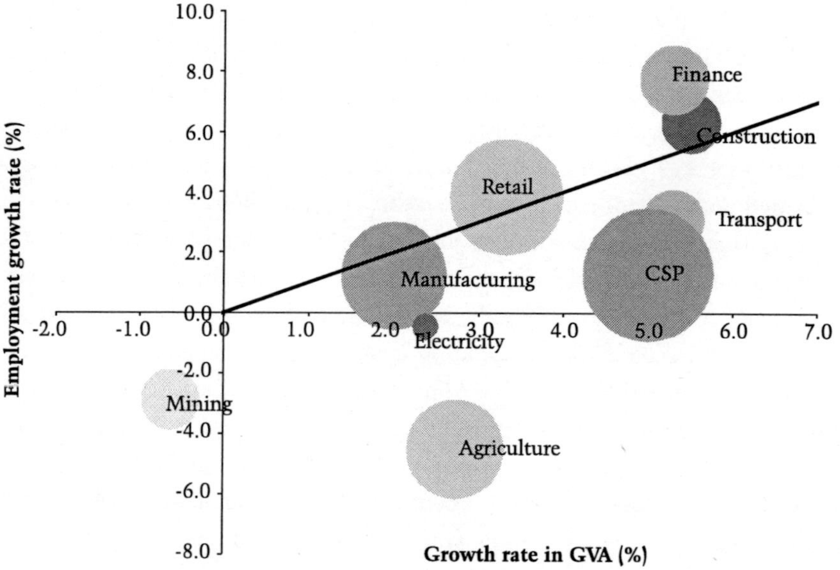

Notes: 1. Constant 2005 prices. 'Community, Social and Personal (CSP) services' include domestic workers in private households, and individuals whose sectors were insufficiently defined or unspecified, or who are classified as working in the 'Exterior organizations and foreign government' sector.

2. For each sector, the rate of growth of real gross value added and the rate of sectoral employment growth are used for the co-ordinates of the centre of the relevant circle. The size of each circle represents the relative size of employment in that sector in 1995. Thus, a large circle represents a sector employing more people than a smaller circle. The graph can be divided into four quadrants. The upper right quadrant is characterized by both GVA and employment expansion, while the lower left quadrant contains sectors where both GVA and employment have been in decline. In the lower right quadrant, GVA is growing but employment is declining, while the opposite is true of the upper left quadrant. Further, the 45° line divides the graph into two sections. The upper section represents points where employment expansion is more rapid than GVA expansion, while the lower section represents points where employment expansion has been slower than GVA growth. Naturally, on this line, employment growth and GVA growth are identical. The interpretation of these two areas can be extended further and conclusions may be reached regarding the labour intensity of gross value added and labour productivity. For example, GVA in a sector above the 45° line has become more labour-intensive over the period, since employment has grown more rapidly than GVA. Put differently, such a sector would have seen GVA per worker decline over the period. The opposite is true for sectors below the 45° line, which would have seen a decline in the labour intensity of GVA or a rise in GVA per worker.

Source: OHS 1995; QLFS Quarter 3, 2009 (Statistics South Africa). GVA growth rates from StatsSA.

Collectively then, the results here suggest that, outside of the primary sectors, most sectors of the economy, whilst increasing employment, have not become more employment-intensive in their growth. Ironically, the only sector which has become marginally more labour-intensive is the financial and business services sector, though this clearly is a reflection of the growth of temporary employment services in this sector.

Sectoral Trade Flows and Employment: The Employment Intensity of Exports

South Africa embarked on a process of trade liberalization in the mid-1980s, intensifying this considerably during the post-apartheid period under World Trade Organization (WTO) commitments. There was, therefore, a significant reduction in the average tariff rates, combined with a simplification of the tariff structure (Cassim, *et al.*, 2002; Edwards, 2006). Evidence, in turn, indicates that this liberalization process has resulted in a twin process of growth in exports and increased import penetration ratios. Furthermore, studies have shown that increased trade over time in South Africa is significantly associated with a growth in total factor productivity, with little evidence, if any, of de-industrialization (Cassim *et al.*, 2002; Tsikata, 1999). However, the debate within South Africa on trade reform during the post-apartheid period has also focused on the labour market effects. Tariff reduction seems to have been disproportionately applied to labour-intensive sectors, with the growth in net trade during the post-1994 period biased strongly in favour of skill-intensive sectors (Edwards, 2006). A more detailed decomposition exercise designed to measure the sources of employment growth during the post-apartheid period, however, finds a small positive effect on employment from net trade, with many of the employment losses in the formal sector attributable to technological change. Perhaps one of the key determinants of trade performance during the first decade of democracy has been the exchange rate. There has been a significant increase in the volatility of the real effective exchange rate since 1994, which has resulted in considerable uncertainty amongst exporters (Cassim, *et al.*, 2002). Given that monetary policy is now guided by inflation targeting, the exchange rate has ceased to be a nominal anchor, and hence the search for a stable and competitive exchange rate becomes a key variable for export competitiveness in the future.

We attempt below, more modestly, to reflect on the relationship between trade and employment, by estimating simple elasticities of employment-exports for the period 1997-2008 at the sectoral level. Specifically, we attempt to assess the relationship between the growth of exports and the change in employment for the tradable good sectors as well as a range of manufacturing sub-sectors.

Figure 5.3 presents the simple ratio of growth rates in employment relative to growth in export volume, as measured by the value of exports, for the period 1997-2008 within agriculture, mining and manufacturing, together with the change in the real effective exchange rate over the period (a rise on the graph in exchange rates indicates appreciation).

Two key results are evident from the above. Firstly, in 2004 the decline in the elasticities for both agriculture and mining was due to a continuing decrease in employment levels, while exports grew modestly in both sectors. Over the same period, the real effective exchange rate continued to appreciate, but at a much slower rate than in 2003. In both these cases, the fairly small growth in exports was not driven by a weaker exchange rate and actually took place while the local currency continued to strengthen, albeit at a slower pace. For these two sectors, there is thus no clear evidence that exports are significantly sensitive to real effective exchange rates. Here it appears as if the growth effects from foreign demand outweigh the negative price movements via the exchange rate. Secondly, and perhaps more importantly for our purposes here, the results suggest a fairly modest relationship between employment and exports. Whilst we explore the linkages between trade and employment in more sophistication below, the results show for example that over the period 1997-2008, for every one per cent growth in export volume, employment increased by 0.40 per cent at the median for mining. The estimate for agriculture was negative, suggesting job attrition as exports expanded over the period, though the employment intensity of manufacturing exports was positive, as the former increased at the median by 1.66 per cent for every 1 per cent rise in exports. However, as we illustrate below, despite this aggregate manufacturing performance, the four-digit level performance was distinctly uneven.

The evidence in Figure 5.4 shows that only four of the 27 manufacturing sub-sectors (included in this four is 'other manufacturing') in the South African economy reported an employment expansion in excess of export volume growth over the seven-year period, as shown by the high and positive elasticity estimates. Furthermore, the largest employers within manufacturing, including wearing apparel, food and beverages, and basic non-ferrous metals, all yield low employment-export simple

Figure 5.3

The Employment Intensity of Exports and the Real Exchange Rate, 1997-2008

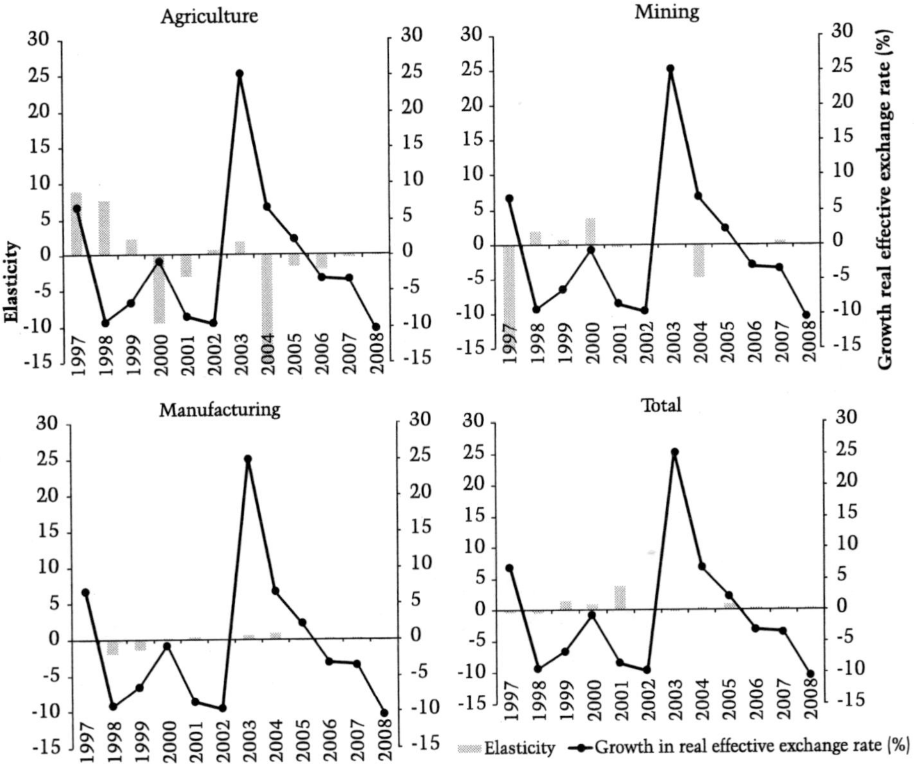

Notes: 1. Elasticity estimates are 'simple elasticities', calculated as the ratio of the annual growth rate in employment to the annual growth rate in the total value of exports.

2. All values are at 2010 prices.

Source: Quantec Data (2008) and own calculations.

Figure 5.4

The Employment Intensity of Manufacturing Exports, by Employment Share within Manufacturing, 2001-2008

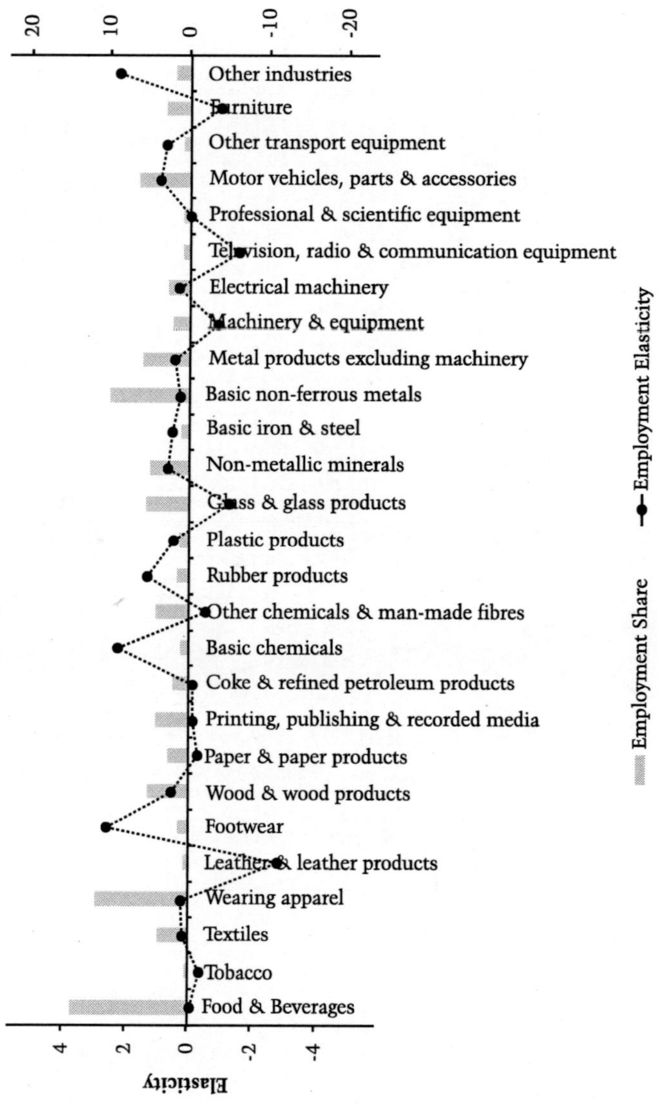

Note: All values at 2010 prices.

Source: Quantec Data (2008) and own calculations.

elasticity estimates. Any notion of a high export growth strategy within manufacturing as a direct first-round effect towards creating employment is surely, therefore, questionable with these data.

The Impact of Trade Flows on Labour Demand, 1995-2005: A Decomposition Analysis

One of the major challenges in looking at the impact of trade flows on the South African labour market is, of course, to unravel the specific impact of tariff liberalization, as opposed to a range of other factors such as the exchange rate and domestic demand, on employment patterns. What we attempt here is an examination of the impact of the change in trade flows on labour demand through the use of a decomposition technique, first utilized by Katz and Murphy (1992). The methodological approach of the technique is contained in Appendix 1.

Essentially, the technique proceeds from the assumption that labour, as a factor of production, is required to produce goods and services. Given this, changes in output or production levels would induce changes in the demand for labour. Net exports constitute tradable output that utilizes domestic labour. We isolate the value of net trade in national output and measure the contribution of labour identified by occupation, race and gender to this traded output. The results indicate how far different types of labour are positively or negatively affected by the movements in net trade.

The two drawbacks of this technique are that we assume relative wages to be constant and that the long-term multiplier effects on employment are not considered, as the technique cannot predict whether continued growth in net exports may, in fact, benefit those skills-defined cohorts that initially lost out from the change in trade volumes. This is, of course, an important component of the debate around the costs and benefits of trade liberalization. However, while not providing such a dynamic long-term analysis, the decomposition provides useful results about the short- and medium-term labour demand trajectory that trade flows are likely to engender.

We assume that the demand for production and non-production workers is affected to a similar extent through exports and imports. One must keep in mind that if this is not the case, and if more highly skilled workers are not displaced through imports to the same degree as production workers, then the change in relative demand for these occupations (the production workers) would be understated in our calculations. The underlying sectoral data that informed the calculations are drawn from only two sectors: manufacturing[1] and mining. Trade data on services remain problematic. The agriculture sector was omitted completely from the decompositions (both in terms of the underlying sectoral data and the employment estimates) because the creation of a new occupation group, skilled agricultural and forestry workers, after 1995 and the re-classification of those workers make comparisons of employment in that sector highly problematic. The manufacturing and mining sectors, however, continue to constitute the dominant share of exports and imports in the South African economy, so these decompositions are still meaningful.

Figure 5.5 presents the results for the trade flow decomposition by occupation group between 1995 and 2005. The results suggest that both highly skilled workers (managers and professionals) and unskilled workers (elementary and domestic workers)[2] enjoyed positive relative demand due

Figure 5.5

Shifts in Relative Demand due to Trade by Occupation

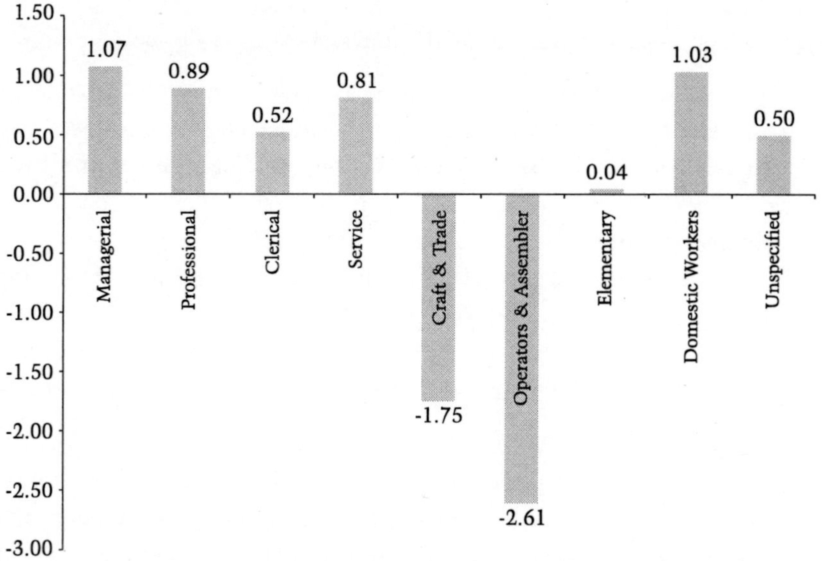

Source: OHS 1995, LFS 2005(2) (Statistics SA) and authors' own calculations.

to trade over the decade. Managers, however, benefited the most, with elementary workers experiencing only a very small relative increase in demand.

The experiences for semi-skilled workers vary across categories. Clerical and services workers experienced relative increases in demand due to trade, while craft and trade workers, as well as operators and assemblers, experienced a sharp decline in relative demand as a consequence of trade flows during this post-1994 period. The results generally suggest that skilled workers and certain semi-skilled categories benefited from international trade between 1995 and 2005, while production workers (as represented by craft and trade workers, and operators and assemblers) suffered the most. This may, in part, reflect the decline of certain import-competing manufacturing sectors, such as clothing.

The trade flow decomposition by race (Figure 5.6) shows that only Africans experienced a relative decline in the demand for their labour. This is not surprising, as Africans have relatively high representation in those

Figure 5.6

Shifts in Relative Demand due to Trade by Race

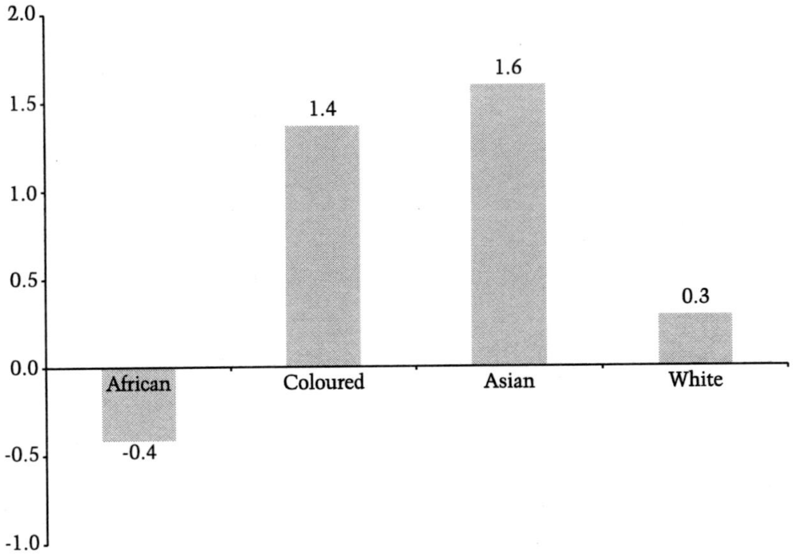

Source: OHS 1995, LFS 2005(2) (Statistics SA) and authors' own calculations.

two occupation groups that experienced a relative decline in demand for labour over the period.

These results are broadly consistent with the occupational labour demand responses, indicating that skilled workers gained from trade flows since 1994, whilst lesser skilled (disproportionately African) workers witnessed a decline in their employment as a consequence of trade.[3]

Whilst the data are not shown here, the trade decompositions by gender indicate that males experienced a decline in relative demand for their labour, while females experienced a relative increase in demand for labour due to trade. This may partly be a reflection of males losing jobs in the mining and manufacturing sectors. This result is corroborated by the evidence above (Table 5.2), of increased feminization of the labour market since 1995, as well as by the fact that women benefited more from the new jobs created over the decade.

Finally, Figure 5.7 shows the impact of trade flows on the demand for labour by level of education. It can be seen that trade had a positive effect on those with a relatively higher level of education.

Figure 5.7

Shifts in Relative Demand due to Trade by Education

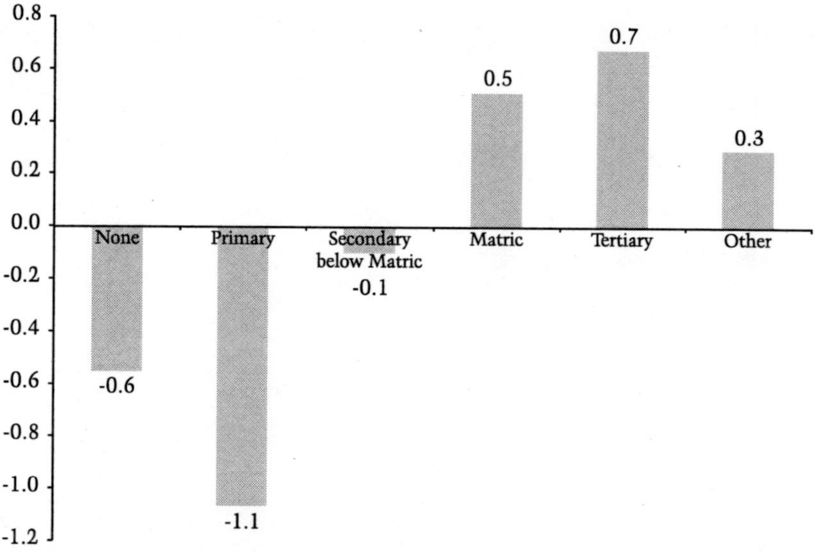

Source: OHS 1995, LFS 2005(2) (Statistics SA) and authors' own calculations.

The increased demand for skilled labour is clear. The three lower education groups, including individuals with some secondary education (but without Grade 12 schooling), experienced a decline in their relative demand for labour. Tertiary educated individuals benefited most from the increase in labour demand due to trade. The skills-biased nature of labour demand patterns in mining and manufacturing, as a consequence of trade flows since 1995, is thus evident here.

To summarize, the winners in terms of increased demand for labour as a result of international trade between 1995 and 2005 have generally been highly skilled, and to a certain extent, semi-skilled workers. The losers were African and male workers, who are generally over-represented in the production worker categories that experienced job losses due to trade.

Returns to Human Capital and Household Income Inequality

The evidence from employment shifts when a combination of cells is examined—be they education, sector or occupation—do suggest that South Africa's labour demand trajectory since 1994 has continued to be skills-biased in nature. We assess below whether the returns to education and skills also reflect this quantity shift. If so, the differential returns to human capital must remain critical for understanding both individual level and household income inequality in South Africa. We turn to both these nodes of income inequality in what follows below.

Returns to Human Capital

Labour market data from industrialized countries tend to display an increase in both the relative wages of skilled (tertiary education) to unskilled (high school education or less) workers, as well as in the ratio of employment for these workers across time (Katz and Murphy, 1992). Figure 5.8 presents the ratios of the real monthly wages of skilled workers in South Africa relative to unskilled workers (W_s/W_u) as well as the ratio of skilled to unskilled employment (N_s/N_u) in 2001 and 2007.[4] Skilled individuals are defined here as those with a tertiary education, whilst unskilled individuals are those with a Grade 12 education or lower.

Figure 5.8

Skilled–Unskilled Relative Wages and Employment, 2001-2007

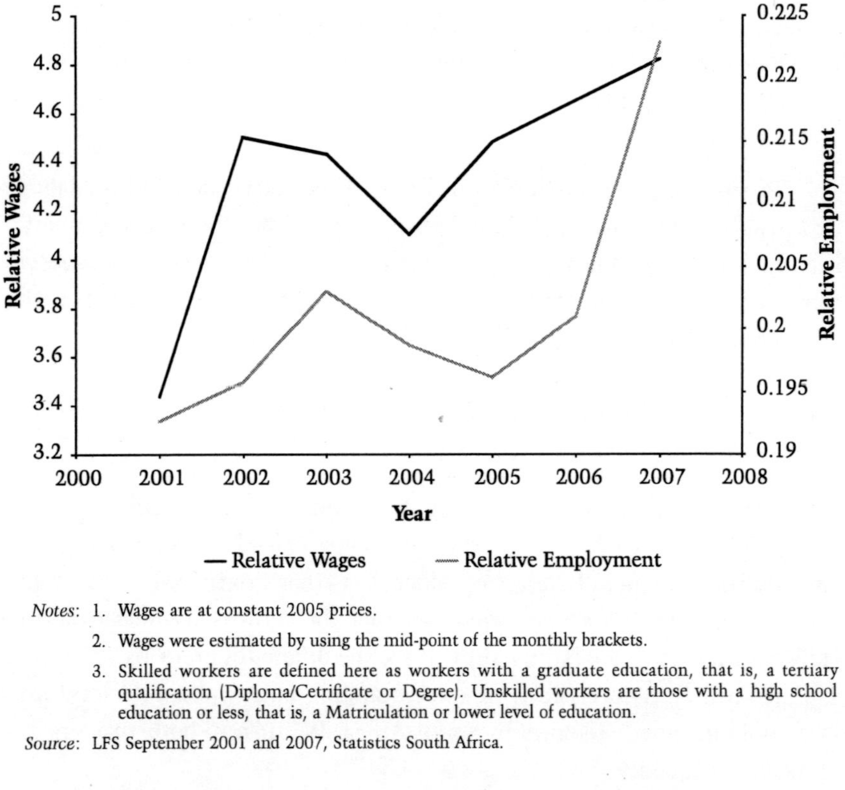

Notes: 1. Wages are at constant 2005 prices.

2. Wages were estimated by using the mid-point of the monthly brackets.

3. Skilled workers are defined here as workers with a graduate education, that is, a tertiary qualification (Diploma/Cetrificate or Degree). Unskilled workers are those with a high school education or less, that is, a Matriculation or lower level of education.

Source: LFS September 2001 and 2007, Statistics South Africa.

Figure 5.8 is visually powerful as it suggests very clearly that over the period 2001 to 2007, both the ratio of (skilled–unskilled) wages and the concomitant ratio of skilled–unskilled employment rose. Specifically, the results show that the ratio of real monthly wages of skilled to unskilled individuals increased significantly between 2001 and 2007 at the rate of 4.38 per cent per annum, whilst the relative employment of skilled individuals rose by 4.67 per cent.

This key result, as previous evidence for developed countries confirms (Katz and Murphy, 1992), is strong evidence of the presence of skills-biased technical change within a labour market. Hence, the evidence here would seem to suggest that the South African labour market continues to deliver disproportionate employment (and concomitant reward) for skilled workers.

In Table 5.5, we present schooling coefficients taken from earnings functions for all employed individuals for 2007. We report the standard OLS results. In all the estimations, earnings are measured by the log of the monthly wage earned by each employed individual. The educational variables are splines corresponding to the years of education completed.

The positive returns to education are evident from the results below, with additional years of schooling (presented by the education splines) impacting positively on earnings, to the point of a diploma, beyond which there is a decline in the mean. Specifically, the data indicate that whilst incomplete schooling attracted a return, on an average, of between 3.5 and 6.6 per cent per additional year of schooling in 2007, this increased sharply with complete secondary schooling and beyond. For example, conditional on finding employment, a high school completion certificate is associated with a mean return of 22 per cent. Notably, this is higher than the average return to some higher educational qualification.

Table 5.5

Returns to Schooling: Earnings Function Estimates, 2007

Education Level	*Coefficients*
None-Grade 8	0.035***
Grade 9-11	0.066***
Grade 12	0.220***
Diploma	0.405***
Degree	0.209***
Household Education	0.156***

Notes: 1. *** P<0.01, ** p<0.05, * p<0.1.

2. Controls included, but not reported are: race, gender, age, sector occupation, experience, experience squared, union status, log of hours and province.

3. The estimates here use the broad definition of the labour force.

4. The educational level variables are splines and hence there is no excluded class.

Source: LFS 2007 (Statistics South Africa), own calculations.

Whilst the degree coefficient is lower, we would argue that this cohort of individuals is under-sampled in all data sets, and is more than likely to be an under-estimate of the true returns to higher education. The highest return, on average, though is for those individuals with some form of non-degree post-schooling qualification. Here, the return at the median of the distribution is about 41 per cent—almost double that for those with a degree or Grade 12 qualification. The strong demand for semi-skilled workers during this recent growth period in the South African economy may explain this result. The quantile results affirm the trends in the OLS coefficients, though notably, the results suggest that for those individuals with a diploma, returns at the 10th and 90th percentiles are lower than at the median, suggesting that for these individuals, an additional level of education beyond matriculation makes more of a difference at the mean than at the tails of the distribution.

By including the combined household years of education, we attempted to capture the intergenerational influence of the education of the household heads on the earnings of other family members. The results are fairly consistent with the education splines. An additional year of household education translated into improved average earnings (15.6 per cent).

Ultimately though, these earnings function results for South Africa, using the most recently available wage data from the Labour Force Survey, are consistent with the employment analysis above, in that the economy since 1994 has been marked by a strong bias in labour market trends towards highly educated and skilled workers.

Economic Growth, Employment and Education: Exploring the Interactions

Beyond the descriptive and econometric overview of employment, unemployment and wages given above, it is important to assess in greater detail the nature of South Africa's growth performance. Which education (and therefore implicitly skills) cohorts have gained or lost from this period of unprecedented post-apartheid economic growth? In a sense, what we present below is another methodological approach for examining the nature of South Africa's skills-biased labour demand trajectory and its consequent impact on household inequality in the society. We start by investigating the impact of growth on employment and whether or not the level of educational attainment played a role in the distribution of employment gains in the South African labour force. The aggregate output–employment elasticity estimate for South Africa over the 2001 to 2007 period stands at 0.6. This implies that a 1 per cent increase in output is associated with a 0.6 per cent increase in total employment, reflecting a high level of sensitivity of employment shifts to economic growth. Here, it is particularly interesting to try and understand how this simple elasticity varies when the employed are categorized by education levels. By doing so, we begin to understand whether or not the process of economic growth has delivered equal employment gains to workers across the education continuum.

Figure 5.9

Output–Employment Elasticities, by Education Level, 2001-2007

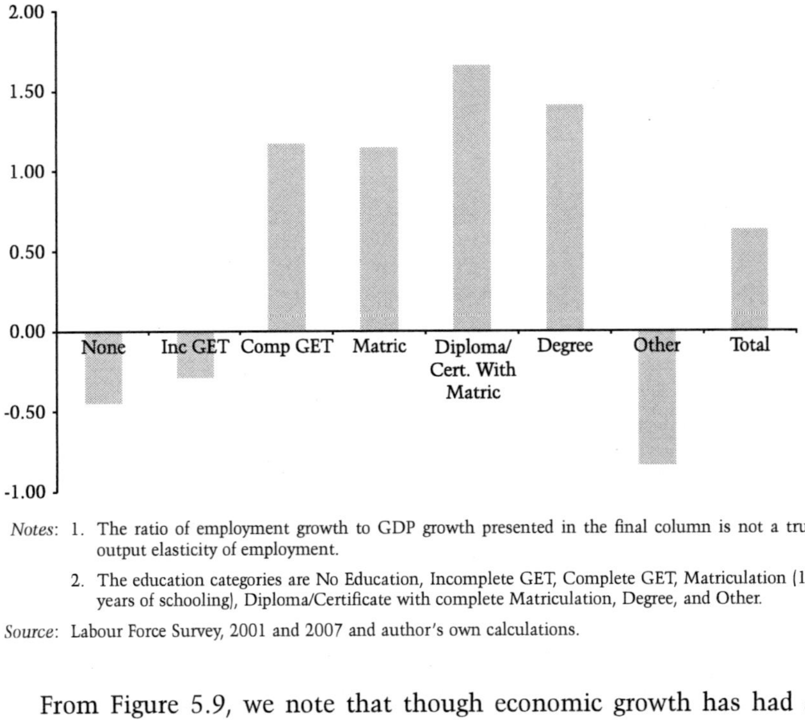

Notes: 1. The ratio of employment growth to GDP growth presented in the final column is not a true output elasticity of employment.

2. The education categories are No Education, Incomplete GET, Complete GET, Matriculation (12 years of schooling), Diploma/Certificate with complete Matriculation, Degree, and Other.

Source: Labour Force Survey, 2001 and 2007 and author's own calculations.

From Figure 5.9, we note that though economic growth has had a positive impact on total employment, the gains from growth in output have been skewed towards the better educated. This is evidenced by the positive elasticity estimates for those with a Complete GET (General Education and Training) qualification or higher. In contrast, the output-employment elasticities for those with no education or an Incomplete GET are negative (-0.45 and -0.29, respectively). In contrast, better-educated individuals benefited from growth over the period, as evidenced by the positive output-employment elasticity estimates for a Complete GET, Matriculation or Tertiary qualification. For instance, a one per cent increase in output yielded a 1.4 per cent increase in employment for individuals with a Degree qualification. These results are consistent with the skills-biased growth trajectory of the South African economy found in previous studies (Bhorat and Hodge, 1999).

While examining the relationship between economic growth and education in more detail, we try to estimate the percentage change in expenditure across the percentile-defined distribution of households according to the level of education of the household head.[5] Hence, Table 5.6 assesses the measures of expenditure growth across five education-categorized groups of households, namely, No education, Incomplete GET, Complete GET, Matriculation, and Tertiary. The growth rates reported below are annual growth rates in per capita expenditure for the period 1995 to 2005. By examining the pattern of gains by level of education of the household head, we note that, for each level of education up to Grade 12, the mean percentile growth rate lies below the national mean of 4.76 per cent. Notably, only tertiary-educated households return a mean growth rate above the national aggregate for the period 1995 to 2005.

Table 5.6

Measures of Growth in Expenditure by Education Level of Household Head, 1995-2005

	None	*Incomplete GET*	*Complete GET*	*Grade 12*	*Tertiary*	*All SA*
Growth rate in mean	4.93	4.74	2.93	5.45	9.57	7.29
Growth rate at median	4.82	3.69	2.01	1.87	9.24	3.78
Mean percentile growth rate	4.6	3.89	2.03	2.52	8.54	4.76

Note: The expenditure growth rates are average annualized growth rates in per capita expenditure. The mean percentile growth rate is the average annualized growth rate in per capita expenditure calculated across all percentiles.

Source: Income and Expenditure Survey (IES), 1995 and 2005.

The picture that emerges from a preliminary analysis of the above results is that the income gains from employment have been concentrated overwhelmingly amongst households headed by individuals with higher levels of education. For example, the mean percentile growth rate in households where the head had a tertiary qualification (8.54 per cent) is almost double that in households headed by individuals with no education (4.6 per cent), and more than twice that in households with heads with an Incomplete GET, Complete GET, or Grade 12 qualification. The mean and the median expenditure growth rates also follow a similar pattern, with much higher growth rates for tertiary-headed households relative to households with lesser-educated heads.

The large and positive per capita expenditure growth rates recorded for households where the household head had a lower level of education (No education and Incomplete GET), relative to households where the head had a complete GET or a Grade 12 qualification, may be further explained by examining the demographics of these households. In particular, lesser-educated households may be older households, and households with lower levels of education and older household heads are more likely to receive income in the form of grants than households where the head has a Grade 12 or a tertiary qualification (where the main source of income is likely to be wage income). Results from the IES 2005/06 showed that grant income was more important than wage income in 72 per cent of the households where the head was uneducated. In contrast, in tertiary-headed households, wage income was the main source of income for most households (92 per cent). Furthermore, given that lesser-educated households in the low-income bracket tend to be older households, income from Old Age Pension grants is likely to be an important source of income in these households. Indeed, the IES showed that in 2005, 12 per cent of households where the head had no education were pensioners, while for households headed by individuals with a Grade 12 or a tertiary qualification, this proportion was much lower, at 1.5 per cent. The low expenditure growth rates recorded for households where the head has a Grade 12 qualification may be attributed to the low income growth recorded by those households in the first place, as well as the insignificance of grant income in these households.

Ultimately though, our expenditure growth estimates suggest that growth during the first decade of democracy has benefited tertiary-educated households more than households headed by any other education cohort. In turn, at the mean, it is in fact Grade 12-educated household heads and those with a Complete GET, who appear to have benefited the least from growth over the period 1995 to 2005. While positive economic growth has been realized, it is evident that not all education cohorts have gained to the same extent. Indeed, these estimates suggest that when abstracting from the labour market sorting that occurs inevitably by human capital attributes, the returns to economic growth in general, and income in particular, are severely biased against individuals and households that do not have some form of post-schooling qualification. This suggests a growth path that is biased towards the better-skilled and educated in the labour market, which contributes to the widening of overall inequality.

In order to shed some light on the low Grade 12 growth rates, Growth Incidence Curves were used to plot the differential in the per capita expenditure growth rates at each percentile between Grade 12-headed households and households where the head had no education. The results obtained are shown in Figure 5.10. We would normally expect this differential to be positive, suggesting a higher growth rate for those with higher levels of schooling. However, for most of the distribution, the graph obtained lies below the origin—an unexpected result. The graph suggests that across most percentiles in the distribution, there has been lower growth in returns at the household level for a completed Grade 12 qualification relative to no education at all. In other words, there are declining returns

Figure 5.10

Household Expenditure Growth Rate 1995-2005:
Grade 12:No Education Household Head Differential

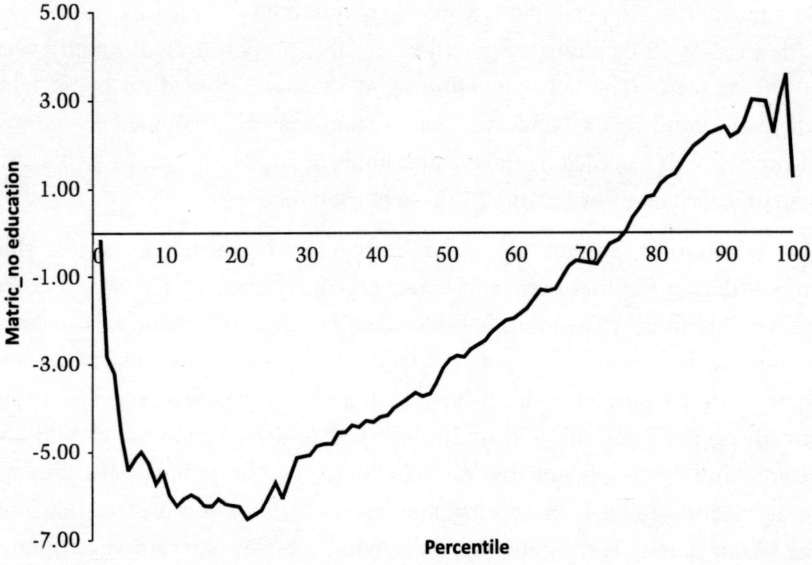

Source: Calculations using IES 1995 and 2005.

to schooling for the first 75 percentiles. This result alludes to the failure of the schooling system in South Africa in generating income growth and progression. This is an extremely powerful result, as it suggests that the completion of 12 years of schooling did not increase returns in terms of growth in the income of this household head, relative to a counterpart head with no schooling at all.

It is only at the tertiary level that the increasing returns to education become evident. Figure 5.11 shows the differential in per capita expenditure growth by percentile in tertiary-headed households versus Grade 12-headed households. For most of the distribution, this differential is large and positive, reflecting the increased gains from accumulating human capital beyond the schooling system.

Figure 5.11

Increasing Household Returns from Tertiary Education versus Grade 12, 1995-2005

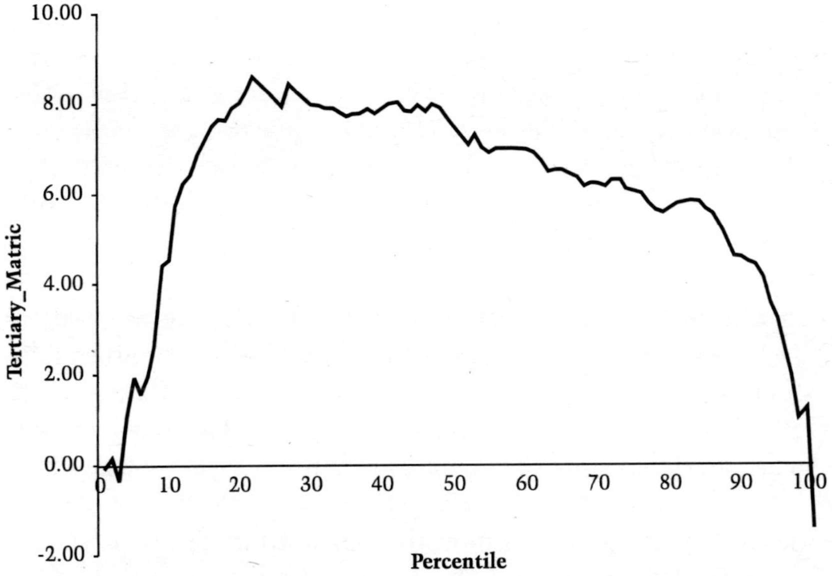

Source: Calculations using IES, 1995 and 2005.

These results then, albeit in a different manner, confirm the labour supply results derived above, which indicated increased returns to higher education. Both the relative wage growth rates for educated workers and, to some extent, the earnings function estimates confirm that high wage premiums are offered to semi-skilled and skilled workers in the South African labour market. The evidence here, which abstracts from the employment status of individuals and examines human capital accumulation at the household level instead, is consistent with one of the recurrent themes in this study—namely that households with tertiary qualifications have gained the most during the post-apartheid period. In addition, the data for households show that when wage and non-wage income accruing to households was considered, Grade 12-educated households did less well than those with zero years of schooling.

Viewed collectively, then, the results derived above reinforce the notion that over the period 1995 to 2005, whilst there has been incomes growth at the national level, this has been unevenly distributed across human capital covariates. In particular, those household heads with some secondary schooling, or indeed, complete secondary schooling, have witnessed the economic growth process deliver either lower or declining returns compared with lesser-educated household heads. These results reinforce the notion that labour demand patterns in South Africa have been characterized by a rise in the relative demand for skilled and semi-skilled workers relative to the unskilled. Since the supply of individuals with these characteristics is constrained, this has resulted in significant higher returns to those with some form of post-schooling qualifications. The latter has arguably engendered a growth path that is heavily skewed towards the better-skilled and educated. This, in turn, has contributed to the inordinately high levels of income inequality witnessed in South Africa during the post-apartheid period. However, it can be argued that these high levels of inequality would indeed have been worse without a key defining attribute of the post-1994 period in South Africa, that is, the importance of social protection measures through the Government. It is to this issue that we turn in our final section.

Social Protection and Economic Growth in South Africa: Social Protection to the Rescue?

The first decade of democracy was characterized by a rapid widening and deepening of the State social security system. Social grants are targeted at the most vulnerable members of the South African society, specifically the disabled, the aged, and children.

An analysis by Pauw and Mncube (2007) shows that not only has the share of social grant expenditure in GDP increased significantly since the first democratic election, but that the number of recipients of social grants has also increased more than three-fold. In 1996/97, social grant transfers accounted for about 2.5 per cent of the GDP; by 2005/06, this share increased to more than 3 per cent. The total number of beneficiaries increased from approximately 3 million in 1997 to 9.4 million in 2005, a total increase of 217 per cent or an average annual growth rate of 15.3 per cent. Table 5.7 illustrates the growth in the number of beneficiaries according to the type of grant.

Table 5.7

Growth in Number of Grant Beneficiaries, by Grant Type, 1997-2005

Type of Grant	*1997*	*2005*	*Change*	*Growth Rate*
Old Age	1,742,253	2,093,075	350,822	2.3%
War Veterans	11,495	3,340	-8,155	-14.3%
Disability	754,830	1,307,459	552,629	7.1%
Grant in Aid	9,720	23,131	13,411	11.4%
Foster Care	42,917	2,56,325	213,408	25.0%
Care Dependency	3,815	85,818	82,003	47.6%
Child Support	400,599	5,633,647	5,233,048	39.2%
Total	2,965,629	9,402,795	6,437,166	15.5%

Note: The child support grant was introduced in 1998, the 1997 beneficiaries shown in the table therefore correspond to the child maintenance grant. Growth rates are average annual growth rates and were calculated by using the estimates for the period 1997 to 2005.

Source: Pauw and Mncube (2007); own calculations.

The increase in the provision of social grants was driven mostly by the extension of the Child Support Grant to children up to the age of 14 years and increased public awareness of the grant (Pauw and Mncube, 2007). The number of recipients of this grant increased from 400,000 in 1997 (when it was called the Child Maintenance Grant) to 5.6 million in 2005, and by 2005, Child Support Grant recipients accounted for almost 60 per cent of all social grant recipients. While the increase in the number of recipients of the Old Age Grant was relatively small, the grant had the second largest number of recipients, with more than 2 million individuals receiving this type of social transfer by January 2006.

Figure 5.12

Household Access to State Grants per Household Income Deciles, 1995 and 2005

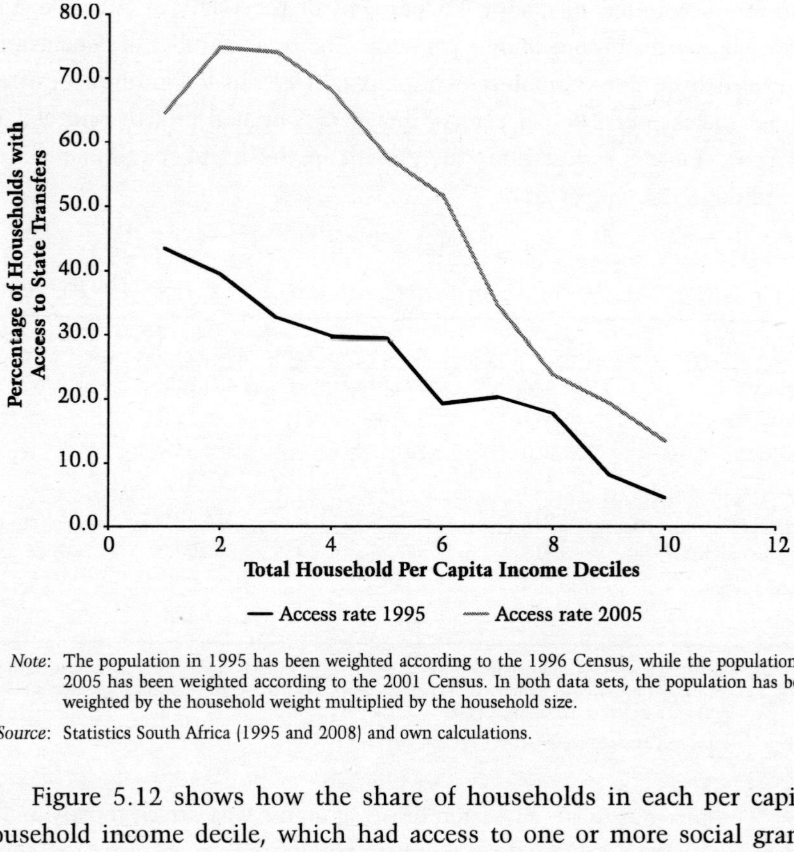

Note: The population in 1995 has been weighted according to the 1996 Census, while the population in 2005 has been weighted according to the 2001 Census. In both data sets, the population has been weighted by the household weight multiplied by the household size.

Source: Statistics South Africa (1995 and 2008) and own calculations.

Figure 5.12 shows how the share of households in each per capita household income decile, which had access to one or more social grant, increased between 1995 and 2005. Put differently, the graph presents the household access rate to social grants in each income decile for the two years under study.

There has been a substantial increase in household access to social grants in each of the income deciles between 1995 and 2005. For example, the share of households in the first decile with access to grant income increased from 43 per cent in 1995 to almost 65 per cent in 2005. However, access to grant income increased significantly not only in the bottom deciles, but also in the deciles in the middle of the income distribution. For example, in the 6th decile, the share of households with access to grant income increased from 19 per cent in 1995 to more than 50 per cent in 2005. This is an important result, which suggests that grant income supports not only the very poor, but also a large portion of households in the middle of the distribution. In fact, between 50 and 75 per cent of the households in the bottom six deciles of the distribution received grant income in 2005. It is worth noting, however, that the access in the bottom decile was smaller than in deciles 2 to 4. This decile includes the unemployed, who do not qualify for grant income.[6]

Figure 5.12 shows the impact of the provision of social grants in terms of the share of households with access to social grants. Figure 5.13 shows which share of total income in each of the total household per capita deciles can be attributed to social grants in 1995 and 2005. It is clear that in line with the increase in access to social grants, the contribution of grant income to total income has increased significantly over the period under study.

In 1995, the contribution of grant income to total household income was relatively low in all deciles. Even in the bottom decile, grant income only contributed about 35 per cent to total income. This contribution declined across the income distribution, with grant income accounting for just more than 10 per cent of total income for those in the fifth decile. By 2005, social transfer income had become an important contributing source to total income in all the lower income deciles. For households in the bottom three deciles, grant income contributed between 50 and 60 per cent to the total household income. We have seen earlier that more than half of the households in the middle of the income distribution received some grant income in 2005. The results above confirm the importance of social grant income to those households, with these social transfers accounting for almost 40 per cent of the total income of households in the 5th income decile.

The proposition, therefore, on the basis of the preliminary evidence gathered here, is that the rapid widening and deepening of the State's social security system during this first decade of democracy lies at the heart of the rapid growth in expenditure levels of the poor. As the above results show, those households at the bottom-end of the distribution experienced large growth rates in expenditure, which was driven by increased access to social grants. The Child Support Grant, the Old Age Pension and the Disability

Figure 5.13

Per Capita Grant Income as a Proportion of the Total Household Income, South Africa, 1995 and 2005

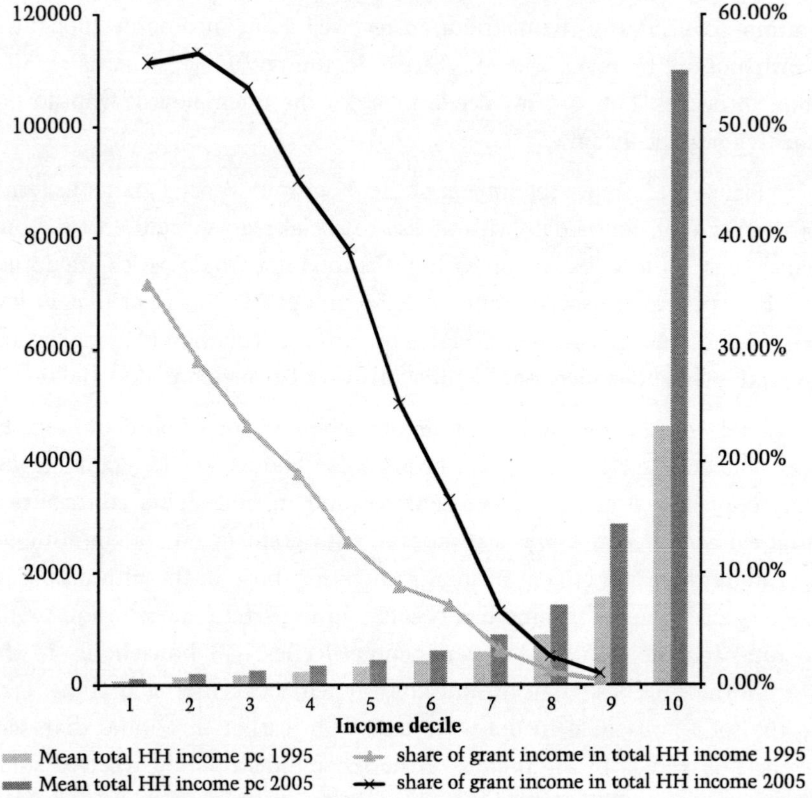

Note: The population in 1995 has been weighted according to the 1996 Census, while the population in 2005 has been weighted according to the 2001 Census. In both data sets, the population has been weighted by the household weight multiplied by the household size.

Source: Statistics South Africa (1995 and 2008) and own calculations.

Grant are thus probably the key individual determinants for South Africa experiencing absolute levels of pro-poor growth during the period 1995-2005. This growth at the bottom-end, however, was accompanied by phenomenal non-social transfer-related growth rates observed amongst individuals from the 80th percentile onwards. These households were the primary direct beneficiaries of South Africa's positive growth rates since 1994.

Conclusion

Ultimately then, our detailed analysis of employment, unemployment and wages suggests a number of broad conclusions regarding the post-apartheid South African labour market. Firstly, in terms of employment shifts between 1995 and 2009, our evidence, in debunking the notion of jobless growth once again, suggests that the domestic economy has created over 3.2 million jobs. Crucially though, this has been insufficient relative to the number of new work-seekers with the consequence being a rise in narrow unemployment rates over the period. Additionally, we show that within these employment trends, since 1995, both an Africanization and a feminization of employment have occurred. More importantly perhaps, it is clear that a labour demand pattern characterized by the disproportionate employment of the better-educated and skilled continues to be a strong feature of this economy. Our sectoral results allude to a key outcome, namely that the vast majority of jobs since 1995 have been created in the financial and business services and the wholesale and retail trade sectors whilst shedding large swathes of primary sector jobs. Within the financial and business services sector, however, it has been the rapid rise in crime prevention services and employment agencies that has driven employment. This is true not only in this sector, but in the aggregate as well.

While examining the impact of trade on employment, we find little evidence to suggest that export growth is associated with an increase in employment. Indeed, there is little evidence within manufacturing, mining or agriculture that historical growth rates in exports have been associated with increased employment levels. Our trade decomposition analysis suggests that where trade flows did create employment, this was principally for educated, skilled workers, who were most likely to be non-African and female. In short then, trade in goods and services cannot be said to have been employment-enhancing within the South African economy since 1994.

Our analysis of labour market inequality suggested firstly, that there is strong evidence of skills-biased employment shifts in the labour market, as both relative wages and employment of skilled workers increased over this period. Secondly, the earnings function results suggest that employers are most likely to pay high levels of remuneration to individuals with post-schooling qualifications. This latter result is then re-asserted with evidence at the household level showing that it has been those household heads with only secondary schooling, or indeed, incomplete secondary schooling, who have experienced a lower growth in returns relative to lesser-educated household heads. It is only at the tertiary level that a higher growth in returns to education is experienced. This suggests that the growth path has been heavily skewed towards the better-skilled and educated. Indeed, a more detailed analysis of the linkages between social protection and wages in the country's growth path suggests that gains from growth are accruing predominantly to individuals (and households) at the top-end of the distribution, that is, the better-educated. This has generated a severely unequal growth path, which has been diluted primarily by one counter-balancing feature, the rapid widening and deepening of South Africa's social security system. South Africa now arguably possesses one of the best-developed social protection systems, amongst the cohort of all middle-income economies in the world. It is this social protection system which has not only ensured a less unequal growth path since 1994 for South Africa, but has also simultaneously raised questions and issues around the sustainability and desirability of such a growth and development path for the country.

References

Bhorat, H. and J. Hodge (1999). "Decomposing Shifts in Labour Demand in South Africa", *South African Journal of Economics* 67(3): 155-68.

Bhorat, H. and C. Van der Westhuizen (2011). *Pro-poor Growth and Social Projection in South Africa: Exploring the Interactions*. Unpublished report prepared for the National Planning Commission.

Cassim, R., D. Onyango, and D.E. Van Seventer (2002). *The State of Trade Policy in South Africa*. Johannesburg: Trade and Industrial Policy Secretariat.

Edwards, L. (2006). "Trade Liberalization and Labour Demand in South Africa during the 1990s", in H. Bhorat and R. Kanbur (2006), *Poverty and Policy in Post-Apartheid South Africa*. Pretoria: HSRC Press.

Katz, L.F. and K.M. Murphy (1992). "Changes in Relative Wages, 1963-1987: Supply and Demand Factors", *Quarterly Journal of Economics* 107(1): 35-78.

Pauw, K. and L. Mncube (2007). "The Impact of Growth and Redistribution on Poverty and Inequality in South Africa", *Working Papers* No. 96,102. University of Cape Town, Development Policy Research Unit.

Quantec (2008). *Quantec Database on Trade.* Pretoria.

Tsikata, Y. (1999). "Liberalization and Trade Performance in South Africa". Informal Discussion Papers on Aspects of the South African Economy. Washington, D.C.: World Bank.

Notes

1. Average values for the manufacturing sector as a whole were used in the calculations.
2. It may be argued that the employment of domestic workers is not expected to be affected by trade. However, during both years, domestic workers were found to be working within the agriculture and mining sectors. These workers were therefore included in the sample.
3. It is interesting to note that though Africans experienced negative labour demand due to trade, domestic labour demand seems to have favoured African workers, who experienced the highest growth rates in employment relative to other population groups.
4. We only focus here on the wage changes between 2001 and 2007, as wage data for this period are not strictly comparable with data from 1995.
5. Education levels of all the individuals in the household were not available, and hence we resort to an imperfect measure of human capital accumulation within the household.
6. In South Africa social grants are targeted at the most vulnerable members of society who are unable to work, such as the disabled, children, and the elderly. There is no income support for unemployed individuals (Bhorat and Van der Westhuizen, 2011).

Appendix A-5.1

Decomposing the Impact of International Trade on Labour Demand (Katz and Murphy, 1992)

In order to measure this impact of trade flows on labour demand, we utilize a similar decomposition technique to the one outlined above and again draw directly from the methodology of Katz and Murphy (1992). This approach isolates the impact of trade flows on shifts in labour demand over time. Assume that the supply of labour, or factor inputs, is related to output in a standard production function paradigm. It is then possible to extend this and consider the impact of direct labour supply on traded output, ignoring indirect input-output effects. Thus, the implicit labour supply function in trade would be the labour input required to produce traded output domestically. Formally, let I_{it} be net imports in industry *i* in year t, Y_{it} the domestic output of industry *i* in year t, and E_{it} the share of labour units in the economy employed in industry *i* at year t. Therefore, the implicit supply of labour embodied in net imports in any given industry at time t, measured as a fraction of total labour units, is given as $(E_{it}/Y_{it})*I_{it}$.

From this formulation, we can derive a more generalized result, i.e. that of the implicit supply of labour of group *k* contained in net trade in year *t* as a proportion of total domestic labour supply of group *k*. This would be:

$$L_t^k = \sum_i e_i^k E_{it}\left(\frac{I_{it}}{Y_{it}}\right) \qquad (2)$$

where e_i^k is the average proportion of employment in industry *i* made up of workers in group *k* over the specified time period. Using the above, we can then measure the effect of trade on the relative demand for demographic group k in year *t* as:

$$T_t^k = -\left(\frac{1}{E^k}\right)\sum_i\left[e_i^k E_{it}\left(\frac{I_{it}}{Y_{it}}\right)\right] + \sum_i E_{it}\left(\frac{I_{it}}{Y_{it}}\right) \qquad (3)$$

where E^k is the average share of total employment of group *k* over the period under consideration. The first term is the implicit labour supply of the group *k* contained in trade, normalized by the base year employment of group *k*, with the sign reversed to convert this supply shift measures into a demand shift measure. The second term adjusts the demand shift measure so that trade affects only the relative demand for labour in group k.

The above equation, however, assumes that export and import flows affect all workers homogeneously. This may not be the case, and it may be true that skilled and unskilled workers are differentially affected by these trade flows. In order to measure this different impact of exports and imports, the first term on the right-hand side of the above equation is replaced by:

$$-\left(\frac{1}{E^k}\right)\sum_i -\left\{\left(e_i^k E_{it}\left(\frac{X_{it}}{Y_{it}}\right)\right)-\left[p_i^k E_{it}\left(\frac{M_{it}}{Y_{it}}\right)\right]\right\} \tag{4}$$

where X measures exports and M imports, and p^k_i is group k's average share of unskilled workers' employment in industry i over the stipulated period. It is therefore assumed that imports will disproportionately impact on the demand for production-level workers relative to export flows.

Appendix A-5.2

Changes in Labour Supply by Educational Category (Official Definition), 1995 to 2009

Education	*1995*		*Q3 2009*		*AAG*
	000s	*Share (%)*	*000s*	*Share (%)*	*(%)*
None	923	8	527	3	-3.8
Incomplete GET	3,830	33	3,381	20	-0.8
Complete GET	2,723	23	4,972	29	4.4
Complete FET	2,571	22	5,119	30	5.1
Diploma/Certificate, less than Grade 12	109	1	120	1	0.8
Diploma/Certificate, with Grade 12	955	8	1,747	10	4.4
Degree	471	4	941	6	5.1
Other	94	1	197	1	5.4
Total	11,676	100	17,004	100	...

Notes: 1. Working age population includes individuals aged between 15 and 65 years old.

2. 1995 data are re-weighted according to the 1996 Census. Data from 2000 onwards have been re-weighted according to the 2001 Census.

3. The official definition (Statistics South Africa) of the labour force has been used there, that is, discouraged workers are excluded from the labour force.

4. The estimates here employ the 'hybrid labour market' definitions for the OHS and LFS.

Source: OHS, 1995; OHS 1997; LFS, September 2000-2007; QLFS, Quarters 1-4, 2008 and Quarters 1-3, 2009 (Statistics South Africa).

6 Comments and Perspectives

Six authors have contributed short comments to this volume, on the basis of their oral interventions as commentators on the presentations in the panel in Dharwad. Some of these comments are broad reflections on the issues discussed in the panel, while others are more specific reactions to the papers presented. They have in common an effort to raise ideas and orientations which merit more analysis in a comparative perspective, and could thus inform the development of collaborative research across emerging economies.

Barbara Harriss-White

As with so many of the exciting new attempts to bring together knowledge about the BRICS, more generally, and to build a comparativist project based upon them, the ambitious papers in this volume would challenge any discussant: responding to the same brief, their theoretical approaches differ as do their empirical foundations and their substantive narratives. While there are rural labour surpluses in Brazil, India and South Africa, brute unemployment structures the South African economy. While India's informal economy is huge—*the* economy—and growing, and is dominated numerically by self-employment, South Africa's is rather modest and confined for the most part to wholesale and retail trade, and Brazil has embarked on a process of re-formalization in the twenty-first century such that its informal economy is relatively one-third the size of India's. We need to understand the extent to which what we compare and contrast are the result of ground realities, or due to the theoretical filter through which the narratives are selected and developed, or due to the way in which the economy has been carved up—and the data delivered—in the national accounts classifications, as also the economic censuses and field material by means of which the informal economy is defined and estimated.

My comments are restricted to two aspects of this huge topic: jobless growth, and barriers to social protection. Most of my comments are informed by the Indian case.

Jobless Growth

In his presentation on Brazil during the Dharwad panel discussion, Barbosa noted the "astonishing presence of self-employment" in the labour markets. Indeed liberalization has unleashed an explosion of tiny one-person firms, which doubled in India between 1990 and 2005. According to the Economic Census (Government of India, 2008), no less than 95 per cent of India's set of 'enterprises' employed no more than five workers in 2005. Firms which are tiny, poor and unable to accumulate constitute the commonest form of production. In conditions of jobless growth in the formal sector, these are the jobs that are created.

The proliferation of terms for this most prevalent kind of work[1] conjures up a Tower of Babel, strongly suggesting the absence of a consensus on how their role is to be theorized. It is clear that self-employment is not a mode of production, it is a *form* that co-exists with others, within a given sector, and/or alongside wage work at a given stage of production and/or in a given region. It competes with various forms of production by using wage labour and generating economics of scale; it is not transitional; it is not a pristine object to be developed. Instead it is the result of a kind of development; it is the backbone of the Indian economy. It is *not* 'not modern'; it is as modern as the corporation and accounts for a greater proportion of GDP than the corporate sector.

One major difference between South Africa, Brazil and India lies in the scope and roles of self-employment: in South Africa, it accounts for a quarter of the informal economy, in Brazil 40 per cent, and in India, for 53 per cent of all livelihoods. Clearly, it drives the development of India's informal economy but there is no consensus on how this kind of work will, or ought to evolve. This is because self-employment embodies capital as well as labour. It is flexible enough to embody many logics of production and exchange. The literature records fixed income objectives; the logic of labour with self-employment regarded as disguised wage work; self-exploitation and super-efficiency with returns that are below wages; flexible deployment for shock-resilience; exploitation on multiple markets (those for premises, raw materials, money, finished products) as compared with wage workers' exploitation on one. Exchange relations involving other kinds of capital prevent accumulation (savings and productive investment). Profit-making is countered by forces preventing profit-making, which are not confined to the market, but also including domestic and collective obligations. Instead of firms growing and employing wage labour, self-employment expands through multiplication.

The State has been accused of neglecting its 'invisible other' (Chakrabarti *et al.*, 2009); but an alternative way of evaluating the policy history of self-employment might be summarized as follows: it is very visible but lacking in coherence. Social protection for the unregistered workforce (discussed below) is but one of its forms—operating outside the sphere of productive work. The State's agrarian populism is another, fallen on stagnant times; its projects for small and medium enterprises (SMEs), micro-enterprise and the 'tiny' sector constitute a third dimension. Micro-finance is a fourth. Inclusive development (based increasingly on identity rather than workforce status) is a fifth. While it hardly needs mentioning that such approaches are under-funded, what is more significant is that the State's development projects are riddled with contradictions. Super-marketization and city beautification displace self-employment; micro-finance and municipal market infrastructure promote it; social safety nets of all kinds protect it (even if protecting self-employment is not their deliberate objective); indirect taxation tolerates it; enforced minimum wages threaten it by incentivizing wage labour but they also represent an unintended opportunity by being a floor below which self-employment can self-exploit. Obviously the balance of policy forces can vary significantly from place to place. However, self-employment and jobless growth, India's competitive advantage, do not constitute a scenario for development that is "friendly to labour".

Since self-employment is suspended between capital and labour, it is hardly surprising that its politics suffers similar contradictions to its development project. As capital, petty producers may be incorporated into farmers' movements and business associations but their interests lie at the foot of the agenda. As labour, self-employed workers are regulated as 'disguised wage labour', though their access to legal claim is thwarted when a single employer cannot be identified—they are then 'de-classed' (Sankaran,

2008). Petty production 'for itself'— acting in its own interests—is championed by the wide variety of productive activities and infrastructural services undertaken by the Self Employed Women's Association (SEWA). SEWA, however, has benefited from donor funding, and, despite its real achievements, covers only 1/200th of the workforce. Lastly, the politics of identity maps on to sub-populations of the socially disadvantaged self-employed and wage workers, but it does not as yet constitute an economic project for them. Nonetheless, without economic and political projects, the self-employed are not invisible nor do they show any sign of obsolescence.

Social Protection and the Barriers It Faces

The UNRISD Report *Combating Poverty and Inequality: Structural Change, Social Policy and Politics*, launched in September 2010, conceives of Anti-poverty Policy and Human Development Policy as a class of social policy that serves as "economic policy for labour". It is, therefore, diminished when it is classified as a policy field separate from development policy. Social protection has synergy with industrial policy just as the latter has synergy with environmental policy. Emphasizing the point that the relation between industrial policy, work, labour markets and social policy is vital, the UNRISD report pursues these synergies. However, the regulation and recognition of work status does not necessarily guarantee entitlements through work. As explained earlier, the self-employed are classified as labour by labour economists and lawyers, but they forfeit labour rights if they cannot identify an employer (and self-employed producers commonly engage with more than one employer). When social protection cannot be linked to work status, entitlements to social protection have to be derived from citizenship instead. But, following T.H. Marshall, citizenship is a process rather than a category, a process that is long, incomplete, class-stratified and controlled by the State by means of labelling, classification and rationing. It is also championed by civil society through a host of organizations, movements and non-governmental organizations (NGOs) that struggle for operationalized rights, claims, access and accountability, and against forces opposed to their agendas. As Barbosa and Moretto's paper makes clear, the types and quality of social protection exist in tension between the power of the working classes against forces that set out to weaken them and the relative power of the (welfare/developmental) state.

In my comment I want to argue that one of the biggest forces weakening social protection for working people is the process of commodification.

It is generally agreed that the drivers of economic growth are threefold. First, competition adds to the flows of commodities through cost-reducing technical and organizational change. Second, invention creates altogether new commodities. Third, commodification transforms non-commodities into commodities. The domestic sphere, the commons, the body and the State have all been targeted for commodification during the twentieth and twenty-first centuries. I will focus on the State. The commodification of public goods and services requires four political processes to be successfully set in motion. First, human behaviour needs to be turned into a commodity form. (When the health service is commodified, we have to be sick in a form that is recognizably commodifiable.) Second, human needs must be transformed into effective demand. Either the consumer pays or the State pays the provider. Third, production is for profit not for social goals, and productive activity without profit is not undertaken. Fourth, the State must reduce and stabilize the risks encountered by capital as it penetrates and commodifies a sector, as well as the risks subsequently shed by capital in the search for profit.

When a public service is commodified, a set of additional costs is inserted into its provisioning. First, a level of profit must be added to the cost structure, which must be equal to, or exceed, the rates of return elsewhere, otherwise capital would abandon the activity. Second, a set of transaction costs covering negotiation, supervision, monitoring, enforcement and re-negotiation of contracts must be inserted. Third, co-ordination costs between a multiplicity of private firms will add to the structure of costs and make it more complex. The impact of this process on labour must involve direct reductions in its security, in the quality of physical work conditions, in the hours of work and in the levels of pay together with the indirect deterioration in labour security due to the use of labour-displacing new technology.

The private provision of a public service generates a distinctive form of politics as well. In conceding public services and fields of social policy to private providers, the State cannot avoid creating a social structure of private interests. Private capital supplies not only the provisioning of the public service but also comes to dominate the supply of a set of rare policy skills and policy advice because the State, confined as it is to a regulative role, either never possessed them in the first place or no longer possesses them. Rapidly, an epistemic community is consolidated in a way that bridges State and market, and must put profit before the public interest. Policy alternatives are confined to those compatible with the necessarily profit-oriented values of this trans-institutional epistemic community. In the field of social policy, where formal commodification is as prevalent in advanced countries as informal commodification is in developing ones,[2] a number of special contradictions can be observed. For these fields of profit to persist, the problem they address must not be solved. Values other than commercial ones (the Hippocratic Oath, the vocation of education, care in the community, etc.) must be embedded in commercialized labour forces. Management has to encourage these non-commercial values in their workers, and yet they must be subordinated to profit or expressed in stylized ways that are consistent with shareholder value (for example, corporate social responsibility [CSR]).

The process of commodification extends to the core functions of State bureaucracies. Policy-making is re-classified in order for its stages and processes to become commodifiable. (Social) policy can be out-sourced to competing think-tanks operating in quasi-business modes, or to tiers and hierarchies of consulting agencies, with each taking profit while working through relations of patronage. Skilled labour working for private profit without pensions or health provisions would produce public policy for these social fields. (Social) policy can be, and is, "in-sourced"—by means of embedded advisers who are funded privately by the very sector that has to be regulated in the department of the government mandated to regulate it. Serious conflicts of interest are then institutionalized, with the effects ranging from rubber-stamping to predation on a weakened State. Then policy decisions are no longer subject to democratic debate; policy procedures are outsourced to private legal drafting companies and the law becomes a commodifiable resource. Revenue-raising through taxation, which along with aid and borrowing funds policy implementation, is not formally commodified, though bribes to enable fraud (tax evasion) generate far more leakages from the State than do bribes for informally privatized services.[3] When it comes to access, India's flourishing literature on corruption has explored the re-ordering of access through bribes, through the commodification of public positions and services (capitation, fees, etc.) and through the private purchase and resale of under-priced public assets.[4] Meanwhile, the scholarly literature on human development has noted the asymmetries between measures supportive of capital including exceptions to sovereignty, on the one hand, and "economic policy for labour". Social policy is under-funded and becalmed in the legislative doldrums on the other. Meanwhile 'accountability' is no longer a social value, but is commodified as a set of quasi-audit practices and outsourced to global management consultancies.

Clearly, the commodification of policy weakens the developmental and transformative powers of the State. The development of social protection, in particular, and social sector policy, in general, requires the de-commodification of the public sphere. There are, therefore, lessons to be learnt from the BRICS, not only for other BRICS but also for Western European countries.

Dipak Mazumdar

In their presentations, the authors of the papers said that all the four countries, *viz.*, Brazil, India, China and South Africa, have the common feature of being labour-surplus economies. The implications of labour surplus relevant to the growth process is that the major 'traditional sector' has a 'non-capitalist' structure à la Lewis, that is, labour in this sector is not paid according to the 'capitalist' mode of profit maximization with the wage equated to the marginal product of labour, rather the sector is characterized by work and consumption-sharing so that labour earns the average product in the sector. An economy like this is likely to experience large inter-sectoral earnings differences as the marginal product of labour in the developing or modern sectors is well in excess of the average product of labour in the traditional sector. Hence, such economies are prone to experience a significant increase in inequality during the growth process.

The trend towards growing inequality would be strengthened if growth in the developing sectors were to be skill-intensive. This seems to have happened in the manufacturing growth of Brazil and South Africa, and in the tertiary sector growth of India. China, however, is characterized by the strong growth of labour-intensive manufacturing exports similar to that experienced by the East Asian economies—Japan, Taiwan and Korea—during their growth process. Yet China has experienced growing inequality contrary to the experience of East Asian growth. More research and thought is needed to throw light on this difference. Is the different type of size structure in manufacturing, with China being skewed to the large enterprise rather than the more even size distribution seen elsewhere in East Asia, responsible, at least partly, for this difference?

Turning to social assistance/protection measures, the authors of the Brazilian paper made the point that Brazil has been particularly successful in recent years in taxing the income of the skilled to subsidize the income of the unskilled. This is indeed what social assistance programmes are supposed to do. Why has Brazil been more successful in these measures than India? Is the Indian package of social assistance programmes unsuccessful because of the high dependence of the Indian package on subsidies of various kinds, which have proved to be regressive?

Amilton Moretto

In my comment I will raise some points that are part of the current agenda for discussion in Brazil, or that are of concern to researchers in the world of labour, following the three main themes of the panel.

The Employment Effect of Global Integration

The good economic performance in Brazil during the last decade contradicted the dominant economic theories, which suggested that economic growth could not exceed 3 per cent per year due to intensified global competition and high labour costs. Solutions started to be found to the problem of generating formal wage employment, and then the following issues were put on the agenda:

- How to ensure that economic growth continues during the coming years and sustains the growth of wage employment?
- What public policies can support this growth while maintaining the competitiveness of companies internationally, guaranteeing labour rights, and, a point which came on the agenda more recently, promoting environmental sustainability?

Macroeconomic policy should be capable of responding to these issues, while at the same time maintaining an active social policy, which can integrate the socially excluded.

The Universalization of Social Protection

Given the large contingent of people working without a wage employment relationship in the Brazilian labour market, and considering that access to social rights is built on that relationship; assuming that high growth continues for the next few years, but at the same time knowing that this growth would not generate wage employment for all those seeking a gainful occupation; and considering also that the vast majority of workers excluded from wage employment would be those with less education and lower professional qualifications, the following questions need to be addressed:

- How can we rethink the financing of social security in order to provide social protection for these informal workers?
- In relation to the funding of social protection, what policies can ensure a balance between the social contributions of the most labour-intensive companies (especially of the service sector) and those that are more capital-intensive?

The following question is embedded in the broader and difficult context of the need for a reform of Brazilian tax policy, in order to make it more progressive:

- How can the labour movement have a more prominent role in this vital discussion?

The theme of social protection will gain importance as regional integration progresses—in the Brazilian case, the integrated South American common market, Mercosur. The reason is the need to create mechanisms of social protection for workers who migrate to work in a neighbouring country. This question cannot be ignored for much longer.

Inequality in the Labour Market

Here, the questions pertain to the role of trade unions. The improved economic and employment environment, in recent years, permitted the most organized trade unions to move away from the defensive position they held in the 1990s. Thus, workers' bargaining power has improved, and there have been real wage gains.

However, a significant portion of workers cannot count on strong trade unions that are capable of delivering substantial improvements in terms of wages and in other dimensions of work.

Therefore, alongside the strengthening of unions, it is imperative to develop public policies that contribute to decent work, thereby reducing the inequalities in the labour market. Themes such as gender relations and racial inequalities are issues that require greater attention at a time when the economy is starting to generate more opportunities.

In this context, a fundamental research question is how to improve the capacity of labour relations to decrease the income gap between workers with the same skills.

In our view, it is not just a matter of improving training policies in the framework of public employment services. It is also a matter of building a long-term strategy that can articulate basic education with the labour market.

At the same time, we must think of the short term, because there are at present a large number of individuals, especially adults aged over 45 years, with low education and poor skills. Such situations highlight the importance of labour market policies that support the establishment of the social economy, and provide these workers with the right conditions for their future retirement.

This challenge calls for the development of a set of policies, concerned with social protection as well as social work, that would be able to capture these complex differences in the labour market, and respond to key social questions, including, for instance, the protection of migrant workers, who are largely living illegally and frequently working in slave-like conditions in major metropolitan centres.

Bhajan S. Grewal

These comments concern the paper by Haroon Bhorat, Natasha Mayet and Carlene van der Westhuizen. The authors deal with important aspects of the South African economy since the end of apartheid, while discussing in detail trends in the labour market, growth of the labour force, education and skill levels, employment patterns, unemployment and social protection. The major conclusion of the paper is that the growth of South Africa's economy has not been rapid enough to absorb the growth in the labour force. Although 3.2 million jobs were created between 1994 and 2009, the labour force grew by 4.7 million during the same period, adding further to the already large pool of the unemployed. Indeed, the number of unemployed more than doubled between 1995 and 2009, and the unemployment rate, which has been rising at the average annual rate of 5.2 per cent, reached 28.3 per cent in 2009, one of the highest rates of unemployment among developing countries. Although it has not been mentioned in the paper, the unemployment rates for the youth must be even higher because their share in employment has fallen.

While the number of jobs in the primary sector has fallen, most other sectors have not become more labour-intensive in their growth. Employment growth has also been concentrated mainly in two sectors—wholesale and retail trade, and financial and business services—which are together responsible for two-thirds of the total employment growth since 1994. Three out of four jobs created in the financial and business sector are those for security services and labour brokers. The authors note that the high incidence of crime in South Africa has, in fact, resulted in rapid employment expansion within the sub-sector providing crime prevention services.

In terms of the pattern of demand for labour, liberalization of trade has mainly benefited the skilled workers and females, as the employment shares of both categories have increased. In contrast, trade liberalization resulted in job losses in production worker categories, which employed large numbers of African and male workers.

The picture that emerges from these features of South Africa's economic growth during the post-Apartheid period is quite alarming. The growth rates have clearly been inadequate to absorb the growing workforce. Unemployment, which is already alarmingly high, continues to grow. The African male workers, and households with heads without secondary education have not benefited from economic growth.

The number of recipients of a social protection grant increased from 3 million in 1997 to 9.4 million in 2005, to 13.5 million in 2009. Labour market outcomes have also generated increasing income inequalities. Not only those without education, but also those with only up to grade 12 education seem to have been unable to access gainful employment. As noted by the authors, the high level of inequality might have been even higher if it were not for the growth of social protection programmes.

Against this background, it would be impossible to characterize South Africa's social protection system as anything other than an indicator of failure of economic growth. It is not clear from this paper how the government of South Africa proposes to re-balance the current model of economic growth in favour of one that creates a sufficient number of jobs to reduce unemployment. Nor is it clear whether the rapidly growing fiscal burden of social protection programmes threatens the sustainability of South Africa's public finances. There is indirect evidence that the opportunity cost of the current social protection system in South Africa is already very high and is having a huge adverse impact on budgetary priorities. For example, government expenditure on social grants increased from 3.2 per cent of GDP in 2001 to 4.4 per cent in 2009, while government expenditure on most budget items (for example, education and healthcare) has remained fairly constant in real terms (Leibbrandt *et al.*, 2010). The bigger social grants grow in the future, the more difficult it would become for the government to finance public expenditure on other more productive budgetary priorities.

S. Mahendra Dev

The Broader Issues

The experience during the last two decades has been that in spite of higher output growth, employment growth has been low in the emerging economies. The employment generated in many countries has been more in the informal sectors without social protection. The jobs that are created are of low productivity, with low wages and without social security.

Another issue is that of inequality in the labour market. Inequality has increased in India, China and South Africa. Only in the case of Brazil did inequality decline, and here too only marginally.

There is a need for policies aimed at ensuring more inclusive development. Such policies should promote productive inclusion by supporting labour-intensive production, and increasing wages and incomes in the sectors that are lagging behind, for example, policies that would improve the productivity of small and marginal farmers, and small and medium enterprises. Macro policies such as fiscal, monetary, trade, agriculture and industrial policies should also be designed in the light of the goal of inclusive development.

Unemployment among youth is another problem in many of the emerging countries. India is said to face a window of opportunity created by the 'demographic dividend'. However, the 'demographic dividend' argument ignores the fact that available workers are not automatically absorbed in the labour market. There is a need to address deficits in education and 'employability' of the workforce with skill development and other active labour market policies in order to take advantage of the opportunity of growth that the demographic dividend is supposed to offer to India.

Social Protection in the Emerging Economies

There are two views on social protection. One view is that it is a waste and funds do not reach the poor. Therefore, it is better to focus on rapid growth and to spend more on healthcare and education than on social protection programmes. The majority view, however, is that there is a need to maintain an acceptable minimum floor of social protection for social cohesion and to prevent the irreversible losses of human capital in hard times. Good social protection programmes promote high-return investments by households. We feel that social protection should be seen in the broader sense of social policy rather than mere palliative programmes. Social protection has both intrinsic and instrumental value.

Wage employment programmes like the Mahatma Gandhi National Rural Employment Guarantee Act (MGNREGA) have been relatively successful in India. Most evaluations of MGNREGA show that its implementation has been more effective than that of any of its predecessor schemes. This is because of the introduction of a number of innovations in the design and implementation of the scheme. MGNREGA has introduced a rights-based framework and legal guarantee of work. Transparency and accountability through social audits are important features of the programme.

Beyond MGNREGA, there is a need for social security in the unorganized sector. In India, only organized workers, constituting 8 per cent of the total number of workers, have access to formal social security. The present schemes in the unorganized sector cover only 5 to 6 per cent of the unorganized workers. The National Commission for Enterprises in the Unorganized Sector (NCEUS) argued for a universal minimum social security coverage. This is a controversial issue. Some advocate a widening of the agenda of social policy towards the holistic approach of universal social protection. Some others claim that targeting is a better option. Many countries use conditional cash transfers as the basis for social assistance. Conditional cash transfers that have worked well include the food-for-education programme in Bangladesh, Mexico's PROGRESA programme and the Bolsa Escola in Brazil. However, it is better to move towards universalism in the medium to long run.

In most countries, the effective implementation of social protection programmes poses a problem. There is a disconnect between policies and implementation. There is thus an urgent need to build appropriate institutional structures for better implementation. The adoption of a participatory and rights-based approach, a bottoms-up approach, social mobilization, social audit, and decentralization can help improve the effectiveness of the programmes. It is being increasingly recognized that the use of information technology (IT) leads to better monitoring and implementation of social protection programmes.

There are, however, some barriers to the extension and effective implementation of social protection programmes. These include the lack of resources, economic and social (caste, gender, etc.) inequalities, illiteracy, the prevalence of weak public sector administrative mechanisms and capacities at the local level (for example, panchayats in India), and the low participation of NGOs and civil society. Finally, some of the programmes, like MGNREGA, threaten the existing hierarchies at the village level and lead to resistance from the local elite. These barriers have to be overcome in order to effectively strengthen social protection programmes.

Rizwanul Islam

I would like to start my observations with the premise that one of the basic objectives of development in the emerging economies should be to utilize their surplus labour through industrialization. An important question in this regard would be the degree of success they achieve in the attainment of this goal. A few observations may be made on the basis of the available empirical evidence on the employment and labour market situation in countries like Brazil, China, India, and South Africa.

First, these countries exhibit low and declining elasticity of employment with respect to output growth even though they are still characterized by the existence of surplus labour and the so-called Lewis turning point has not yet been attained. The continued availability of surplus labour in countries like India, for example, is indicated by the high proportion of the employed labour force in the unorganized sector. In South Africa, the rate of open unemployment is very high. As for China, though there is a view that surplus labour has probably been exhausted there, it remains doubtful as to whether this would be the right conclusion if the entire country were taken into consideration. In both China and India, the elasticity of employment with respect to output is not only low but has also been declining, with respect to both overall output and manufacturing. Brazil seems to be an exception to the pattern mentioned above where there was a substantial decline in the rate of unemployment and an increase in real wages during the period 2002-09. The adoption of a counter-cyclical fiscal policy during the year 2008-09 helped the labour market recover quickly from the downturn caused by the Great Recession.

Second, in order to achieve a change in the structure of output and employment that is necessary for ensuring the productive absorption of surplus labour, the manufacturing sector needs to grow at a high rate. The experience of countries which were able to pass the Lewis turning point successfully and quickly (for example, the Republic of Korea, Malaysia, and Taiwan, China) indicates that the elasticity of growth of the manufacturing sector with respect to overall GDP growth needs to be around 1.8 to 2. In India, it was around 1.3 during the 1990s and the first half of the 2000s. Instead of manufacturing, growth of the service sector has been high. As a result, rather than a transformation of the structure of employment from agriculture to manufacturing, the transformation has been from agriculture to services. In South Africa also, the growth of employment in manufacturing has been rather low.

Third, though conventional wisdom suggests that a market-oriented and open economy facilitates export-oriented labour-intensive industrialization (which, in turn, is the path taken by successful late industrializers for attaining industrialization through the utilization of surplus labour), the recent experience of countries like India shows that the relationship between the two is not automatic. In India, since the opening up of the trade regime, the share of labour-intensive industries in total manufacturing value added has not increased. And the export basket has seen increases in the shares of both labour-intensive and capital-intensive industries.

Fourth, in contrast to the experience of countries like the Republic of Korea and Taiwan, China, which were able to attain high rates of economic growth without letting inequality in income distribution worsen, the experience of China, India, and South Africa is the opposite. Only Brazil seems to have been able to prevent a worsening of inequality. One factor that can be observed in the difference in experience between Korea and Taiwan, on the one hand, and between China, India and South Africa, on the other, could be the poor performance on the employment and labour market front. In the latter, wages have often lagged behind the growth of labour productivity. In India, the gap between wages and returns to labour in the formal and informal sectors appears to have increased. Moreover, higher education is associated with higher returns; and progress in education has been far from equitable.

Fifth, in trying to explain the poor performance of countries like India on the employment and labour market front, rigidities in the labour market are often cited as the major factor, and the importance of the incentive structure that prevails in the factor market is almost never considered. And yet, a careful examination of the situation points out that distortions in relative factor prices may remain even in market-oriented economies. In India, for example, policies aimed ostensibly at encouraging investment (for example, subsidy on interest, and measures to facilitate capital upgrading) contain powerful elements that lower the cost of capital. On the other hand, there is almost nothing to encourage the use of labour. And the result is a distortion in relative factor prices that encourage the use of capital.

I would like to conclude by making an observation with regard to the environment in which policies relevant for employment and the labour market are generally formulated in developing countries. In formulating economic policies, the primary (if not the only) goal often is to achieve a high rate of economic growth. Employment consideration is normally added as an after-thought. Economic policy-making thus remains disconnected from measures, if any, aimed at employment and labour market objectives. When employment receives some attention, it is treated separately through special programmes, such as MGNREGA in India, and the Expanded Public Works Programme in South Africa. A strategy for employment and the labour market is, therefore, unlikely to be effective unless it is integrated into economic policy-making.

References

Chakrabarti, A., A. Chaudhury and S. Cullenberg (2009). "Global Order and the New Economic Policy in India: The (Post)-colonial Formation of the Small-scale Sector", *Cambridge Journal of Economics* 33(6): 1169-86.

Government of India (2008). *Economic Census, 2005*. New Delhi: Ministry of Statistics and Programme Implementation. Available at: *http://mospi.gov.in/index_6june08.htm*

Guhan, S. and S. Paul (eds.) (1997). *Corruption in India: Agenda for Action*. New Delhi: Vision.

Leibbrandt, Murray, Ingrid Woolard, Hayley McEwen and Charlotte Koep (2010). "Trends in South African Income Distribution and Poverty since the Fall of Apartheid", *OECD Social, Employment and Migration Working Papers* No. 101. Paris: OECD.

Roy, R. (1996). "State Failure: Political–fiscal Implications of the Black Economy", in Barbara Harriss-White and Gordon White (eds.), *Liberalization and the New Corruption, Special Issue, Bulletin, Institute of Development Studies* 27(2): 22-31.

Sankaran, K. (2008). "Informal Economy, Own Account Workers and the Law: An Overview", WIEGO Law Pilot Project on the Informal Economy. Harvard: Kennedy School.

UNRISD (2010). *Combating Poverty and Inequality: Structural Change, Social Policy and Politics*. Geneva: UNRISD.

Notes

1. Variously: self-employment; non-capitalist production; non-remunerated work in income-generating activities; own account enterprise; household/family production; cottage/tiny industry; micro-enterprise; petty (commodity) production; simple reproduction; sub-proletarians; reserve army; the 'invisible other'.
2. The term 'informal commodification' here refers to the commodification of public goods, sometimes directly, as when rice from the public distribution system (PDS) is purloined and sold on the open market; sometimes indirectly when the G2 bandwidth is under-priced for purchase from the State and then resold for private profit;

and sometimes through substitution as when private night watch and protection substitutes for the police.

3. It may be vulnerable to the design of retrogressive social transfers from labour to capital (which is noticed in India from Panchayat Taxes upwards). For the relative significance of corruption and tax evasion, see Roy (1996).
4. See, for a useful instance, Guhan and Paul (1997).